Bihar: From Ashoka to the Present

Author: Rohan Kumar

Price: 699/-

Author: Rohan Kumar

Titel: Bihar: Ashoka to the Present

ISBN: 978-93-344-3667-9

First Edition: 2025

Self-Published

"I dedicate this book to the people of Bihar, whose resilience, culture, and history continue to inspire me. This book is a humble attempt to trace the journey of Bihar from the glorious Mauryan Empire under Ashoka to the challenges and hopes of today."

— Rohan Kumar

CONTENTS

Chapter 1 — The Rise of Magadh Empire

In the long and layered story of India, there are few places as quietly powerful as Bihar. At first glance, it might not appear as the epicenter of empires, ideas, and revolutions — but peel back the centuries, and a dazzling truth emerges: Bihar, known in ancient times as Magadha, was the beating heart of a civilization that shaped not just India but much of Asia.

This chapter begins not with kings and palaces, but with rivers and soil — because that is where Magadh's story truly starts.

1. A Land Blessed by Rivers and Riches

Long before history was written down, the land between the Ganga and the Son rivers was already thriving. The plains of what is today southern Bihar were fertile beyond measure. Year after year, the rivers brought alluvial soil, nourishing crops and sustaining dense human settlements. Thick forests covered the hills of Rajgir, iron lay hidden beneath the earth, and water flowed through the plains like a blessing.

This was not just good land — it was strategic land. Whoever controlled Magadh controlled the trade routes that crisscrossed the subcontinent: from the Ganga basin to the Bay of Bengal, from the Himalayan foothills to central India.

By the 6th century BCE, small kingdoms called Mahajanapadas were emerging across northern India. Among these — Kosala, Vatsa, Avanti, and others —

Magadh began as just another regional power. No one yet knew that it would outshine them all.

2. Bimbisara: The Visionary King

History often turns when the right land meets the right leader. For Magadh, that leader was Bimbisara. Born into the Haryanka dynasty around 544 BCE, Bimbisara ascended the throne as a young man. But he was no ordinary ruler. He combined the strategic mind of a soldier with the diplomatic vision of a statesman.

Bimbisara expanded his kingdom through both war and marriage alliances. He conquered the neighboring kingdom of Anga, a major center of trade, bringing the rich port of Champa under Magadh's control. To secure his northern border, he married Kosala Devi, the sister of the Kosalan king. To secure the east, he allied with Licchavis of Vaishali.

But his genius lay not just in expansion. Bimbisara shifted his capital to Rajgir (Rajagriha), a natural fortress surrounded by hills. He improved roads, developed administration, and — unlike many kings of his time — maintained regular contact with his subjects.

It was during his reign that Magadh became known as the "Kingdom of Prosperity." Traders, monks, and thinkers flocked to its cities.

Bimbisara was also a contemporary and supporter of Gautama Buddha. It is said that the young Buddha, after enlightenment, visited Rajgir to meet him. Bimbisara offered him land to build a monastery, and that became

Veluvana — one of the earliest Buddhist monasteries in history.

This was the beginning of a unique political–spiritual relationship: Magadh's rulers would shape religions, and religions would shape Magadh's destiny.

3. Ajatashatru and the Age of Ambition

When Bimbisara died, his son Ajatashatru ascended the throne under dark circumstances. Ancient texts differ in their accounts, but many suggest that Ajatashatru imprisoned his father and seized power — a reminder that empire-building is often shadowed by ambition and blood.

Ajatashatru, however, proved to be as formidable a ruler as his father, though more ruthless. His reign marked a turning point: Magadh was no longer content with being a rich kingdom; it now sought to dominate the entire Gangetic plain.

His first challenge was the powerful Licchavi confederacy in Vaishali. Ajatashatru, recognizing the strength of their democratic republic, built a fortified city at Pataliputra (modern Patna), right at the confluence of the Ganga and Son rivers. This city would later become one of the greatest capitals in Indian history.

The war with the Licchavis lasted years. Ajatashatru used military innovations — including a war engine known as the mahashilakantaka, a catapult that could hurl huge stones — to break the confederacy. Eventually, Magadh triumphed. By the end of Ajatashatru's reign,

Magadh controlled vast stretches of northern India. Its capital was secure, its economy was booming, and its rulers had learned to mix force with strategy.

Ajatashatru too had a spiritual side. He supported both Buddhism and Jainism, and his court saw visits from the Buddha as well as Mahavira. Imagine this: a single king hosting the founders of two of India's greatest faiths. Few places in the world can claim such moments.

4. Why Magadh Triumphed Over Others

Why did Magadh, and not other Mahajanapadas, become the nucleus of empire? Historians point to several reasons, and each reveals something about the character of this land:

1. Geography: Bounded by rivers and hills, Magadh was easily defensible yet well-connected. Control of river routes meant control of trade and grain supply.

2. Resources: The presence of iron ore in nearby hills gave Magadh a military edge. Iron tools and weapons allowed it to build stronger armies and clear forests for agriculture.

3. Leadership: From Bimbisara to Ajatashatru, early Magadhan kings were strategic and ambitious. They combined diplomacy, warfare, and administration in ways their rivals could not.

4. Agriculture and Economy: A rich agrarian base meant steady revenue. Trade through the Ganga turned Pataliputra into a commercial hub.

5. Political Vision: While many Mahajanapadas were republics with divided power, Magadh had a strong centralized monarchy. That allowed it to act swiftly and decisively.

Magadh's rise was not an accident. It was the result of geography meeting vision.

5. Pataliputra: The Birth of a Legendary Capital

Around the mid-5th century BCE, Ajatashatru laid the foundations of a city on the banks of the Ganga. It was meant to be a military outpost. But Pataliputra was destined to be more than that — it would become the nerve center of empires for the next 800 years.

Later dynasties — the Nandas, Mauryas, and Guptas — all ruled from here. When foreign travelers like Megasthenes came to India centuries later, they described Pataliputra as one of the largest and most beautiful cities in the world, with wooden palaces, gardens, and bustling markets.

Its location was a masterstroke. It sat at a river junction, giving it both economic vitality and military strength. It was a city that could not be easily besieged.

In many ways, the rise of Pataliputra mirrors the rise of Magadh itself: humble beginnings, strategic growth, and eventual glory.

6. Seeds of Empire: The Nanda Transformation

The Haryanka dynasty eventually fell, giving way to the Shishunagas and then to the Nanda dynasty.

The Nandas, though often portrayed as unpopular, were extraordinary administrators. They built a powerful standing army — some accounts suggest hundreds of thousands of soldiers — and amassed enormous wealth through efficient taxation.

They extended Magadh's boundaries beyond the Ganga plains, bringing almost the entire northern India under their control. Unlike earlier kings who relied heavily on alliances, the Nandas used administrative might and military strength to hold their empire together.

Their centralized bureaucracy, standardized revenue systems, and emphasis on economic control laid the groundwork for something even greater — the Maurya Empire.

When Alexander the Great invaded northwestern India around 326 BCE, his armies heard tales of the Nanda king's power. Even the mighty Macedonians hesitated to march east towards Magadh.

7. Spiritual Crossroads of a Civilization

While power was consolidating politically, something equally extraordinary was happening spiritually. Magadh was a melting pot of ideas.

It was here that Gautama Buddha walked, taught, and gained thousands of followers. His first great monastery was in Rajgir; his followers spread from these plains to all of Asia. It was here too that Mahavira, the 24th Tirthankara of Jainism, preached a message of non-violence and self-restraint. Unlike many kingdoms where rulers feared new religions, Magadhan kings supported both. This was partly political — it allowed them to unify diverse populations — but also cultural. The soil of Bihar has always been porous to ideas; it absorbs and transforms them.

By the time the Mauryas rose, Magadh was not just a military power. It was the intellectual and spiritual heartland of India.

8. Ordinary Lives in an Extraordinary Time

Empires are often remembered through their kings. But the strength of Magadh lay also in its people — farmers, traders, potters, monks, and soldiers.

In the villages, farmers worked the fertile land, growing rice, barley, and wheat. The surplus fed armies and allowed cities to grow.

In the towns, craftsmen made pottery, tools, ornaments, and textiles that were traded across the subcontinent. The Ganga was not just a river; it was a highway of commerce.

In monasteries and forest retreats, monks debated questions of existence and ethics. Travelers and merchants carried these ideas to distant lands — Sri Lanka, Central Asia, and beyond.

Magadh's greatness was collective. It was the outcome of a society that balanced material prosperity with intellectual curiosity.

9. From Regional Kingdom to Empire

By the 4th century BCE, Magadh was no longer just a kingdom — it was the dominant power in northern India. Its capital was the largest city. Its army was the strongest. Its economy was the richest. Its influence stretched far beyond its borders.

The stage was now set for one of history's greatest empires: the Mauryan Empire. But even before Chandragupta Maurya, Magadh had already achieved something rare: it had become the gravitational center of the subcontinent.

Unlike many ancient powers that rose and fell in obscurity, Magadh's legacy was enduring. Its administrative innovations were adopted by later empires. Its spiritual movements changed Asia. Its cities became legends.

10. Legacy of the Rise

When we look back at the rise of Magadh, what stands out is not just conquest but continuity. Magadh managed to build layer upon layer of power — political, economic, cultural — over centuries.

Bimbisara laid the foundation, Ajatashatru built the fortress, the Nandas added might, and the Mauryas would soon bring global fame.

This layered history is why Bihar today, though often spoken of in the context of modern struggles, carries an ancient and proud memory. Every river bend, every mound of earth, every ruin near Rajgir or Pataliputra whispers the same story: this was once the center of the world.

11. A Civilization's First Ascent

The rise of Magadh is not just a chapter in Bihar's history; it is a chapter in the making of India itself.

Here, empire was born not from the coast, not from foreign invasion, but from the deep plains of the Ganga. Here, power and philosophy walked hand in hand. Here, cities were built not just for war, but for learning.

When Bimbisara looked out over the hills of Rajgir, he could not have known how far his kingdom's shadow would stretch. But history remembers. And it begins here, in Magadh.

Chapter 2 — Ashoka the Great: The Emperor of Dharma

History often crowns conquerors with power. But once in a great while, a conqueror crowns history with compassion. In the story of India — and of Bihar — one such figure stands apart: Ashoka, remembered not only as an emperor but as Dharmaraja, the King of Righteousness.

More than two thousand years ago, Ashoka ruled from the heart of Magadh. From his capital at Pataliputra, his empire stretched from Afghanistan in the northwest to Tamil Nadu in the south, and from Bengal in the east to the mountains of present-day Pakistan in the west.

He could have gone down in history as just another great conqueror. Instead, he chose a different path — one that would change the spiritual map of Asia.

1. The World Ashoka Inherited

When Ashoka was born around 304 BCE, Magadh was already the imperial core of the subcontinent. His grandfather, Chandragupta Maurya, had overthrown the Nandas and built the Maurya Empire. His father, Bindusara, expanded it further.

Pataliputra was the jewel of the empire. Foreign travelers like Megasthenes described its massive wooden palaces, broad avenues, and administrative precision. There were spies, tax collectors, record keepers, soldiers, and merchants — a buzzing imperial machine.

But behind the polished order of empire, there were tensions too. Succession battles brewed. Provincial governors eyed power. And in the heart of the royal palace, young Ashoka watched and learned.

2. A Prince of Fire

Ashoka was not his father's chosen heir. Known for his fiery temper and military skill, he was seen by some in the court as dangerous. To keep him away from Pataliputra, Bindusara sent him to govern Ujjain, a distant but important province.

But Ashoka was not easily sidelined. In Ujjain, he proved himself as a capable administrator and a brilliant strategist. When rebellion broke out in the region of Takshashila, Ashoka crushed it swiftly, earning the respect — and fear — of both the army and the court.

Legends say that he was called Chandashoka — Ashoka the Fierce — for his ruthlessness in battle. He was the kind of prince who would not wait for destiny; he would seize it.

3. The Battle for the Throne

When Bindusara died, a bloody struggle for succession broke out among his many sons. Ancient texts differ on the details, but all agree that Ashoka emerged victorious after a brutal fight, possibly killing several brothers in the process.

It was a coronation written in blood. But Ashoka, now emperor at around the age of 30, wasted no time. He strengthened the bureaucracy, consolidated the frontiers, and began to expand the empire even further.

The Mauryan Empire, already vast, became the largest political entity India had ever seen.

4. Kalinga: The Turning Point

If there is a single event that changed Ashoka's life — and the history of India — it is the Kalinga War.

Kalinga (modern Odisha) was an independent, prosperous region on the eastern coast. It controlled vital trade routes and refused to bow to Magadhan power. Ashoka, determined to bring it under imperial control, launched a massive military campaign around 261 BCE.

The war was brutal. Kalinga's soldiers and civilians resisted fiercely. When the dust settled, the land was soaked in blood. Ancient inscriptions record that 100,000 people were killed, 150,000 were deported, and countless others perished in famine and disease that followed.

For the first time, the victorious emperor did not feel triumph. He felt horror.

Ashoka rode through the battlefield after the war and saw corpses piled high, rivers red with blood, families broken forever. In that moment, something in him shifted.Power no longer felt glorious. It felt hollow.

5. A King Transformed

In the aftermath of Kalinga, Ashoka experienced a profound transformation. He turned away from violence and conquest, embracing the path of Dharma — a moral law rooted in compassion, tolerance, and respect for all life.

He became a follower of Buddhism, not as a monk but as a king determined to govern through ethical principles.

"I consider the victory through Dharma to be the greatest victory," he proclaimed in his edicts.

He ordered an end to aggressive wars. He promoted non-violence, built hospitals for humans and animals, and supported Buddhist monks and monasteries. He sent missions to spread the message of Dharma far and wide — to Sri Lanka, Central Asia, and beyond.

This was not weakness. It was a new kind of strength: the strength of conscience.

6. The Edicts of Ashoka: A King's Voice in Stone

We know more about Ashoka than almost any other ancient Indian ruler, thanks to the inscriptions he left behind — the Edicts of Ashoka. Carved into rocks and pillars across the empire, they were written in Prakrit, Greek, and Aramaic — so everyone, from commoners to nobles, could understand. These edicts were revolutionary. Instead of boasting about victories or issuing threats, they spoke about ethics: "All men are my children."

“Let no one think only of their own religion or condemn others.”

“True conquest is through Dharma, not war.”

In a world of emperors who built empires through fear, Ashoka tried to build one through moral example.

His most famous inscriptions were on the lion-topped pillar at Sarnath, which later became the national emblem of modern India.

7. Pataliputra: The Capital of an Idea

Pataliputra under Ashoka was not just the capital of an empire — it was the capital of an idea.

Foreign envoys came to the city and marveled at its beauty. Buddhist monks from across Asia gathered to debate, study, and spread teachings. Hospitals, gardens, rest houses, and irrigation projects were built across the empire.

The emperor’s palace, according to Greek accounts, rivaled the palaces of Persia in grandeur. But Ashoka’s legacy was not in stone buildings alone; it was in the invisible architecture of ethics and governance.

He appointed Dhamma Mahamatras — special officers who traveled the empire, ensuring justice, protecting the weak, and encouraging religious harmony.

8. The Spread of Buddhism: Bihar to the World

From the banks of the Ganga, a spiritual wave flowed outward. Ashoka’s patronage of Buddhism transformed it from a regional faith to a global one.

He supported the construction of stupas, monasteries, and learning centers. Nalanda University and Bodh Gaya became major Buddhist centers.

He sent his own children, Mahinda and Sanghamitta, on missions to Sri Lanka, where Buddhism would flourish for centuries.

The teachings of the Buddha, once confined to Bihar, now traveled along trade routes to China, Central Asia, and Southeast Asia.

Centuries later, travelers in distant lands would still speak of the "great king Ashoka" who spread peace instead of war.

9. Dharma: Not a Religion, but a Way of Life

Ashoka's Dharma was not about forced conversion. He never declared Buddhism as a state religion. Instead, he emphasized principles that transcended faith:

Respect for all religions

Compassion toward living beings

Truthfulness and charity

Good governance and justice

He asked his subjects not to abandon their faiths but to live ethically within them. In a time when empires often imposed their religion, Ashoka's pluralism was ahead of its time. He believed that a kingdom rooted in moral law would be stronger and more lasting than one built by the sword.

10. Ashoka and Bihar: A Sacred Geography

Ashoka's spiritual journey is inseparable from Bihar's geography.

It was in Bodh Gaya, near Pataliputra, that Gautama Buddha attained enlightenment. It was in Rajgir that the early sanghas flourished. It was along the Ganga that Ashoka built pillars inscribed with his moral vision.

His empire was vast, but his heart was rooted in this land. Bihar was not just his power base; it was his spiritual anchor.

Even today, the ruins of ancient stupas, monasteries, and inscriptions in Bihar tell the story of a king who ruled not just with armies, but with ideals.

11. Challenges of a Moral Empire

Ashoka's turn to Dharma did not mean that the empire became perfect overnight. Running such a vast territory was difficult. Not everyone accepted his policies. Some elites resented the emperor's focus on non-violence and religious tolerance.

But Ashoka believed in persuasion, not coercion. His edicts show a patient, almost modern understanding of governance: he asked officials to be gentle with people, to listen to them, to be fair.

His empire lasted long after his death — a testament to the strong administrative and moral foundation he built.

12. The Sunset of a Great Reign

Ashoka ruled for nearly four decades. In his later years, he withdrew more from military affairs and focused on spiritual work.

When he died around 232 BCE, the Mauryan Empire was still powerful, but without his personal vision and authority, cracks slowly appeared. His successors lacked his moral force, and over the next few decades, the empire fragmented.

But Ashoka's Dharma Rajya — his ethical vision of governance — did not die. It became part of India's civilizational DNA.

13. The Emperor Who Became a Legend

Centuries after his death, Ashoka's name faded from popular memory. His inscriptions were forgotten, his pillars buried. But in the 19th century, British archaeologists rediscovered the Edicts of Ashoka. Slowly, the world remembered him again — not as a conqueror, but as a moral visionary.

Today, the lion capital from his pillar at Sarnath is the emblem of Government of India. His wheel of Dharma adorns the national flag.

In a land that has seen countless rulers, Ashoka endures because he was not just a king of men, but a king of ideas.

14. A Different Kind of Greatness

Many emperors build roads. Ashoka built bridges between faiths. Many emperors conquer lands. Ashoka conquered hearts. Many emperors are feared. Ashoka is remembered with love.

He understood something rare: that the real strength of a ruler lies not in the sword but in the moral imagination of his people.

In this sense, Ashoka was centuries ahead of his time — a ruler who replaced empire with empathy.

15. Legacy: Bihar to the World

The story of Ashoka is inseparable from the story of Bihar. From the rise of Magadh to the flowering of Buddhism, Bihar was both the stage and the soul of this transformation.

Through Ashoka, a provincial kingdom became the center of a moral empire. Through Bihar, an emperor's vision traveled across continents.

Today, when pilgrims from Sri Lanka, Japan, or Thailand visit Bodh Gaya, they walk on the same soil where Ashoka once stood.

His empire may have ended, but his Dharma still flows like the Ganga — patient, persistent, eternal.

16. The King Who Chose Peace

If history is a river, then Ashoka is one of its gentlest bends — a place where violence paused, and wisdom flowed.

From a fiery prince to a compassionate emperor, his life is proof that power can transform, that even in the age of empires, there is room for conscience.

And it all began here, in Bihar — the land that made Ashoka, and through him, helped shape a part of the world's soul.

Chapter 3: Nalanda and Vikramshila — Seats of Knowledge

A Golden Era of Learning

In the heart of ancient Bihar, where the Ganga and its tributaries once carried merchants, monks, and philosophers, two magnificent universities arose — Nalanda Mahavihara and Vikramshila Mahavihara. These were not just centres of education; they were crucibles of global knowledge, drawing seekers of wisdom from China, Korea, Tibet, Java, Sumatra, Sri Lanka, and beyond.

Long before modern universities in Europe or America took shape, these Mahaviharas symbolized India's intellectual leadership. They were funded by kings, supported by the public, and run by monks and scholars whose commitment to learning was absolute.

Nalanda, in particular, became a beacon of light during the Gupta period. Its libraries were so vast that they were described as "oceans of knowledge." Vikramshila, established later, became a centre of excellence in Buddhist philosophy and Tantra. Together, they made Bihar the world's classroom.

The Birth of Nalanda: Wisdom Blossoms in Magadha

The origins of Nalanda go back to the 5th century CE. According to historical sources and archaeological evidence, it was founded during the reign of Kumaragupta I of the Gupta Empire around 427 CE.

The choice of Nalanda was not accidental. The region was already sacred to Buddhists. It was near Rajgir, where Gautama Buddha had delivered many sermons, and close to Bodh Gaya, where he attained enlightenment.

The name "Nalanda" is believed to mean "giver of knowledge" (from na-alam-da in Sanskrit). Another interpretation comes from ancient legends — a serpent deity named Nanda protected the region, and so the place came to be known as Nalanda.

Unlike small monasteries or hermitages, Nalanda was a full-fledged residential university. Students lived, studied, and practiced their disciplines there for years. It wasn't just a school of religion — it was a multidisciplinary institution. Teachings included Buddhist philosophy, logic, grammar, medicine, astronomy, mathematics, law, and arts.

Nalanda in Its Prime

At its height, Nalanda housed over 10,000 students and more than 2,000 teachers. The university had eight separate compounds, ten temples, meditation halls, lakes, and parks. It is said that it had three great libraries — Ratnasagara (Sea of Jewels), Ratnodadhi (Ocean of Gems), and Ratnaranjaka (Delight of Jewels).

These libraries held hundreds of thousands of manuscripts, some of which contained advanced mathematical and astronomical theories. Many original Buddhist texts were preserved here, including rare commentaries and translations in Sanskrit, Pali, and local dialects.

Life at Nalanda was rigorous. Admission was not easy — only the most talented students could enter. Historical records from Xuanzang (Hsüan-tsang), a famous Chinese monk who studied here in the 7th century, describe a difficult entrance examination at the main gate, where only a few were admitted after oral questioning by the gatekeepers.

Once admitted, students were immersed in a strict but stimulating academic routine. Discussions and debates were frequent. Scholars were encouraged to challenge ideas, refine arguments, and build logical frameworks. Sanskrit grammar and logic (Nyaya) were taught with precision. Buddhist scriptures were memorized and analyzed in depth.

Nalanda's influence extended far beyond India. Students from China, Korea, Japan, Tibet, Mongolia, Indonesia, and Persia came to study. It became a transnational institution centuries before the concept of globalization existed.

Great Teachers and Visitors

Nalanda produced and hosted some of the greatest minds of the ancient world:

Xuanzang (7th century): A Chinese monk and scholar who traveled over 10,000 miles to reach Nalanda. He spent 5 years studying philosophy, logic, grammar, and Buddhist scriptures. His detailed writings later became an important source of historical information about India and Nalanda.

Yijing: Another Chinese pilgrim who studied at Nalanda after Xuanzang. He praised its discipline and intellectual atmosphere.

Shilabhadra: The abbot of Nalanda during Xuanzang's time, a brilliant scholar who was highly respected throughout Asia.

Dharmapala, Dharmakirti, and Nagarjuna: Legendary philosophers and logicians who developed sophisticated systems of Buddhist thought and logic.

The university was well-supported by successive rulers, including Harsha in the 7th century and the Pala Empire kings in the 8th–12th centuries. Endowments and land grants ensured its smooth functioning.

Vikramshila: A Second Beacon of Knowledge

While Nalanda was already famous, in the late 8th century CE, King Dharmapala of the Pala dynasty founded another great university — Vikramshila. Located near present-day Bhagalpur, Vikramshila rose as a centre for advanced Buddhist studies, especially in Tantric Buddhism (Vajrayana).

Vikramshila was designed in a grand architectural style. A central stupa was surrounded by 108 smaller shrines. The university complex had six large monasteries and hundreds of residential rooms for students and monks. The curriculum focused on logic, philosophy, grammar, metaphysics, and tantric rituals.

The main attraction of Vikramshila was its strict academic discipline. Only the most brilliant students from Nalanda and other Mahaviharas were selected for advanced studies here. This created a two-tiered education system — Nalanda as a foundational university and Vikramshila as a specialized centre.

Scholars of Vikramshila

Among Vikramshila's distinguished scholars were:

Atisha Dipankara Shrijnana: A legendary teacher who played a key role in reviving Buddhism in Tibet. His teachings formed the foundation of Tibetan Buddhism's reformist movements.

Ratnākaraśānti and Jetari: Renowned philosophers who developed sophisticated ideas on logic, epistemology, and meditation.

Naropa: A great teacher who became central to the transmission of Vajrayana Buddhism to Tibet.

Vikramshila was famous not just for its scholarship but also for its international networks. Tibetan monks were trained here, who later returned to their homeland carrying manuscripts and teachings, effectively making Bihar a spiritual exporter of knowledge.

The Nalanda–Vikramshila Network

The Mahaviharas of Nalanda and Vikramshila were not isolated islands. They were part of a network of universities across eastern India — including Odantapuri Mahavihara and Jagaddala Mahavihara.

These institutions maintained intellectual exchanges. Scholars moved from one to another, texts were copied and circulated, and students advanced through the network based on their abilities.

This system resembles modern higher education structures — undergraduate, postgraduate, and research centres — centuries before modern universities in Europe like University of Bologna or University of Oxford emerged.

A Day in the Life of a Nalanda Student

Historical accounts give us a glimpse of daily life at Nalanda. A typical day began at dawn with meditation and recitation. Classes started early, often in open courtyards or lecture halls. Lessons were oral; students memorized texts and engaged in dialectical debates.

Meals were simple, mostly vegetarian, prepared in the university's community kitchens. In the evenings, students gathered for debates or discussions. Teachers, often monks, lived in the same compound, making mentorship a natural part of education.

Libraries were at the heart of the campus. Students spent hours copying manuscripts by hand, ensuring knowledge was preserved and transmitted.

Unlike modern universities, education at Nalanda was free. Kings and merchants funded it through endowments and land grants. Students did not pay fees. In return, they devoted themselves fully to learning and spiritual practice.

The Decline: Fire and Ashes

The golden age of these universities lasted nearly 700 years. But by the 12th century, they faced decline. The fall was not due to lack of brilliance but because of changing political and religious landscapes.

The rise of Hindu kingdoms, decline of Buddhism in India, and invasions from the northwest created a turbulent period.

In 1193 CE, the forces of Bakhtiyar Khalji attacked Nalanda. Historical accounts describe the burning of the great library, which is said to have burned for months. Thousands of manuscripts were lost forever. Monks were killed or dispersed.

Vikramshila faced a similar fate soon after. The universities, once the pride of India, fell silent under the weight of conquest.

This tragedy was not just the loss of buildings but the destruction of centuries of accumulated knowledge. Much of India's intellectual heritage was lost that day.

Legacy Beyond Ruins

Yet, Nalanda and Vikramshila did not disappear entirely. Their teachings and influence survived through their students and manuscripts that had already traveled to Tibet, China, and Southeast Asia.

Tibetan monasteries, in particular, preserved many of Nalanda's teachings. In fact, Tibetan Buddhism today is deeply rooted in the Nalanda tradition. The logical rigor and philosophical debates of Nalanda continue to shape Tibetan monastic education.

Even today, many Tibetan monks refer to themselves as "Nalanda monks."

Rediscovery by Archaeology

In the 19th century, British archaeologists rediscovered Nalanda's ruins. Excavations by Alexander Cunningham and later by John Marshall unearthed brick monasteries, temples, inscriptions, and seals. These findings confirmed the historical accounts of Xuanzang and Yijing.

Nalanda became a symbol of India's ancient intellectual glory. In 2016, Nalanda Mahavihara was declared a UNESCO World Heritage Site.

Nalanda's Rebirth in the Modern Era

In 2010, the Government of India established Nalanda University once again — not as a monastery but as an international university. Supported by several Asian countries, it aims to revive the spirit of Nalanda — global learning, cultural exchange, and intellectual excellence.

Scholars from across the world come to study subjects like history, ecology, philosophy, and cultural studies. While the modern university cannot recreate the ancient one exactly, it carries the same idea: knowledge has no borders.

Why Nalanda and Vikramshila Still Matter

The story of Nalanda and Vikramshila is not just about the past. It holds lessons for the present and the future:

1. Knowledge as a bridge: These universities united people of different lands, faiths, and languages. They show how education can build harmony.

2. Public support for education: Nalanda was funded by society, not private profit. Education was seen as a social good.

3. Academic rigor: Admission based on merit, open debates, and critical thinking made Nalanda great. Modern institutions can learn from this.

4. Resilience of knowledge: Even when burned, Nalanda's ideas survived — because ideas are stronger than walls.

Bihar's Intellectual Soul

For centuries, Bihar has been called "the cradle of knowledge." Nalanda and Vikramshila are its proudest jewels. Their ruins still stand, not as symbols of defeat, but as reminders of how bright the human mind can shine.

The people who walked those brick paths came from distant lands, united by a shared love of learning. They created a world where the search for truth was sacred.

Today, as Bihar rebuilds its education system, these ancient seats of learning offer a timeless vision — that knowledge, when shared freely and pursued with sincerity, can change the course of history.

✨ Epilogue to the Chapter

Bihar's greatness did not come only from empires and rulers. It came from scholars and teachers, from monks who debated under banyan trees, from libraries that welcomed every seeker of truth. Nalanda and Vikramshila represent Bihar at its most luminous.

Their story is proof that civilizations are remembered not by their wars, but by their wisdom.

Chapter 4: Cultural and Religious Heritage of Bihar

The Sacred Land of Many Faiths

Bihar is not just a place on the map; it is a spiritual landscape, a land where some of the world's greatest religions were born, nurtured, and transformed. For over 2,500 years, this soil has carried the footsteps of saints, philosophers, reformers, and pilgrims.

Here, under the shade of a peepal tree, Gautama Buddha attained enlightenment. In these lands, Mahavira gave shape to the doctrines of non-violence and Jainism. It was here that the great Mauryan emperor Ashoka carved edicts on stones, preaching the path of Dharma. It was here that Hinduism, Buddhism, Jainism, Sikhism, and Islam coexisted and influenced each other, giving rise to a culture both diverse and harmonious.

This chapter journeys through that rich cultural and religious tapestry — the rituals, philosophies, festivals, and sacred spaces that have made Bihar a spiritual heartland of India.

The Birthplace of Enlightenment: Bodh Gaya

At the core of Bihar's religious identity stands Bodh Gaya — one of the most sacred sites for Buddhists around the world. Around 5th century BCE, a prince named Siddhartha Gautama from Kapilavastu wandered across northern India in search of truth. His quest ended beneath a peepal tree on the banks of the Niranjana River. Here, he attained enlightenment and became the

Buddha — The Awakened One. The tree became known as the Bodhi tree.

The magnificent Mahabodhi Temple Complex, a UNESCO World Heritage Site, stands as a symbol of that moment of awakening. Its soaring spire, intricate carvings, and the sacred Bodhi tree attract millions of pilgrims each year — from Sri Lanka to Japan, from Thailand to the West.

Bodh Gaya is more than a tourist destination; it is a living spiritual centre. Monasteries from dozens of countries surround the temple complex. The sound of chanting in different languages blends into a universal rhythm of devotion. In this single place, the world's many Buddhist traditions meet.

Jainism's Roots in Bihar

Long before Buddhism spread across Asia, another great spiritual movement was growing in Bihar. Around the 6th century BCE, Mahavira — the 24th Tirthankara of Jainism — was born in Vaishali.

Mahavira's teachings emphasized Ahimsa (non-violence), Satya (truth), and Aparigraha (non-attachment). He walked barefoot across the plains of Bihar, preaching a path of discipline, compassion, and renunciation.

Pawapuri, near Nalanda, is where Mahavira attained Nirvana. Today, the stunning Jal Mandir stands in the middle of a lotus-filled lake at Pawapuri, attracting Jain pilgrims from around the world.

Bihar's landscape is dotted with Jain sites — Rajgir, Champapuri, Kundalpur — each whispering stories of Mahavira's life and the early Jain community. Jainism's philosophy deeply influenced Indian thought and shaped Bihar's cultural fabric of tolerance.

Hinduism: An Ancient and Living Faith

Hinduism has flowed through Bihar for millennia, interwoven with local traditions, folklore, and rituals. The region's epic associations stretch back to ancient India. According to the Ramayana, Sitamarhi is believed to be the birthplace of Sita, the revered consort of Rama. Her story is deeply embedded in the cultural identity of the Mithila region.

Gaya is another ancient pilgrimage site. Long before Buddhism, it was sacred to Hindus. The Vishnupad Temple marks the spot where Lord Vishnu's footprint is said to be imprinted in stone. Even today, thousands perform pind daan rituals here for the salvation of their ancestors' souls. This ancient ritual connects families to their spiritual roots and is considered one of the most sacred acts in Hindu tradition.

Festivals like Chhath Puja — unique to Bihar and parts of eastern India — showcase the depth of Hindu devotion in everyday life. Dedicated to the Sun God, Chhath involves fasting, singing folk songs, and offering prayers at sunrise and sunset. Unlike many rituals, Chhath is led largely by women, emphasizing the central role of women in Bihar's cultural life.

The Arrival of Sikhism: Guru ka Patna

In the 17th century, another spiritual current flowed through Bihar. In 1666, Guru Gobind Singh, the tenth Sikh Guru, was born in Patna. The city became a sacred centre for Sikhs, and the magnificent Takht Sri Harmandir Sahib, Patna (popularly known as Patna Sahib) was built to commemorate his birthplace.

Today, Patna Sahib is one of the five Takhts — the highest seats of authority in Sikhism. It draws devotees from across the world. The Gurudwara's golden domes, serene prayers, and langar (community kitchen) reflect Sikhism's message of equality and service.

Sikhism's presence in Bihar is a testament to the region's openness to multiple faiths. It did not displace existing religions; it became part of the cultural mosaic.

Islam in Bihar: A Sufi Touch

Islam entered Bihar during the medieval period through traders, saints, and later rulers. What flourished here was a Sufi-influenced form of Islam — spiritual, inclusive, and woven into the local culture.

Cities like Maner Sharif became famous for their Sufi shrines. The dargah of Makhdoom Yahya Maneri and Makhdoom Shah Daulat attracted people of all faiths. Sufi saints preached love, brotherhood, and devotion to God without boundaries of caste or creed.

Sufi music, qawwalis, and poetry blended beautifully with local languages, influencing Bihar's folk traditions. Even today, Urs (death anniversaries of saints) are celebrated with devotion, not only by Muslims but also Hindus and others — a living example of interfaith harmony.

Bihar: A Crossroads of Civilizations

Bihar's religious heritage was not just about one faith rising after another; it was about multiple streams flowing together.

Buddhism did not erase Hinduism — it grew alongside it.

Jainism and Buddhism often shared sacred spaces.

Hindu kings supported Buddhist monasteries, and Buddhist rulers respected Hindu temples.

Islam, Sikhism, and Christianity later found their place without displacing the old.

This layered cultural evolution is what gives Bihar its unique identity. In a single town, one may find a temple, a mosque, a Gurudwara, and a monastery — each with centuries of history behind it.

Festivals: The Soul of Bihar's Culture

Festivals in Bihar are not just events; they are living expressions of faith and community.

Chhath Puja: The most iconic festival of Bihar, dedicated to Surya (the Sun God) and Chhathi Maiya. The rituals of standing in the river at dawn and dusk, offering fruits and sweets, and singing folk songs have remained unchanged for centuries.

Diwali and Holi: Celebrated with immense enthusiasm across communities. Holi, especially in Mithila and Bhojpur, is known for its traditional songs and cultural plays.

Ram Navami, Makar Sankranti, and Saraswati Puja**: Reflect deep-rooted Hindu traditions.

Urs at Sufi shrines: Symbolize syncretism. People of different faiths participate in these gatherings with equal devotion.

Buddha Purnima: Celebrated at Bodh Gaya and other sites with chants, lamps, and meditation. Monks and laypersons gather to honor the Buddha's birth, enlightenment, and death on the same day.

Jain festivals like Mahavir Jayanti bring thousands of devotees to Pawapuri and Vaishali.

These festivals show how faith in Bihar is not a private act — it is communal, open, joyous, and shared.

Art, Music, and Literature: Expressions of Faith

Bihar's cultural and religious heritage is also expressed through its art forms.

Mithila or Madhubani Painting: Originating in the Mithila region, this ancient art form was traditionally done on mud walls and floors by women during religious occasions. Today, it is world-famous. Its themes are deeply spiritual — Hindu gods, epics, fertility symbols, and nature.

Folk Music and Bhajans: Religious songs are integral to daily life. Whether it's Chhath songs sung by women at dawn or bhajans during village fairs, music keeps faith alive in simple, powerful ways.

Literature: Ancient texts, such as Buddhist Pali scriptures, Jain Agamas, and Hindu epics, were either written or preserved here. Later, during the medieval era, Sufi poetry in Persian and Urdu flourished, influencing Bhojpuri and Maithili literature.

Philosophical Currents from Bihar

Bihar was not just a place of worship; it was a cradle of philosophical thought.

Buddhism from Bihar spread to the entire world, emphasizing compassion, impermanence, and the middle path.

Jainism taught the principle of non-violence and respect for all living beings.

Hinduism here absorbed folk beliefs, nature worship, and philosophical traditions like Vedanta and Sankhya.

Sufi Islam contributed ideas of spiritual love and divine unity.

This philosophical pluralism made Bihar a model of intellectual and spiritual coexistence. Even today, monks, priests, and scholars from across the world visit Bodh Gaya and Nalanda for dialogues on faith and reason.

Sacred Geography of Bihar

Bihar's geography itself is sacred. Many of its cities and villages are linked to legendary spiritual events:

Bodh Gaya — Enlightenment of the Buddha

Rajgir — Buddha's sermons, Jain pilgrimage

Nalanda — Buddhist learning

Pawapuri — Mahavira's Nirvana

Vaishali — birthplace of Mahavira, first democratic republic

Gaya — Vishnupad Temple, Hindu ancestral rites

Patna Sahib — birthplace of Guru Gobind Singh

Maner Sharif — Sufi shrine

This sacred geography makes Bihar a pilgrimage destination for multiple faiths, bringing together diverse people and beliefs.

Interfaith Harmony and Coexistence

One of the most remarkable aspects of Bihar's cultural heritage is its ability to host many faiths without conflict for long stretches of history.

Even during periods of political change, the common people's faith and rituals remained intertwined. Many Hindu families visit Sufi shrines; Buddhist monks participate in local fairs; Jain and Hindu pilgrims share sacred sites like Rajgir.

This spirit of Ganga-Jamuni tehzeeb — the blending of cultures — remains one of Bihar's most powerful legacies.

Modern Challenges to Heritage

In recent decades, Bihar's spiritual heritage has faced challenges — urbanization, neglect of heritage sites, lack of proper tourism infrastructure, and political indifference.

Many ancient temples, monasteries, and Sufi shrines require preservation. Modernization has also weakened traditional cultural practices in some areas. Yet, the spiritual pulse of Bihar remains strong.

Every year, during Chhath Puja, the ghats of the Ganga River overflow with millions of devotees — a living testament that these traditions are not museum pieces but living heritage.

Revival and Global Recognition

Efforts are now being made to revive and protect Bihar's cultural and religious heritage:

UNESCO has recognized Mahabodhi Temple Complex and Nalanda Mahavihara as World Heritage Sites.

Restoration projects are underway at many Jain and Sufi shrines.

Cultural festivals like the Bihar Diwas celebrations showcase folk music, dance, and religious harmony. Bodh Gaya has become a global Buddhist hub, hosting international conferences and pilgrimages.

Awareness about Chhath Puja has spread globally with the Bihari diaspora.

These efforts point to a new chapter in the story of Bihar's cultural identity.

Why This Heritage Matters

Bihar's cultural and religious heritage is not just about temples, mosques, or festivals. It is about a worldview that values faith, dialogue, and community. It teaches us that multiple religions can grow together. It shows that philosophy and spirituality can shape societies. It reminds us that the identity of a place is not defined by rulers alone but by the faith of its people.

Bihar's contribution to the spiritual history of the world is immense — it gave Buddhism to Asia, Jainism its strongest base, and nurtured Hinduism and Sikhism. It embraced Islam with an open heart. This makes it a rare land of convergence.

✨ Epilogue to the Chapter

Walk through the ghats of Ganga during Chhath, or the courtyards of Bodh Gaya, or the quiet lanes of Maner Sharif, and you will feel the timeless heartbeat of Bihar. Faith here is not a wall but a bridge. It connects past and present, people and philosophy, rituals and reason. In this sacred land, religion has never been just a set of beliefs — it has been a way of living, celebrating, and coexisting. As Bihar moves forward, its cultural and religious heritage stands not as a relic, but as a foundation for unity, pride, and hope.

Chapter 5: The Decline of Ancient Bihar

For centuries, the plains of Bihar had been a beacon of power, faith, and knowledge. Empires rose from its soil, monks carried the Buddha's teachings across continents, and scholars debated philosophy in the halls of Nalanda University and Vikramshila University. But no empire is immune to time. Even the most powerful civilizations face decline—not overnight, but slowly, like a lamp dimming after burning brightly for too long.

1. The End of the Mauryan Glow

The fall began after the death of Ashoka in 232 BCE. Under his reign, the Mauryan Empire had reached its zenith—stretching from Afghanistan to the deep south of India. But Ashoka's successors lacked his vision, administrative skill, and spiritual gravitas.

Internal strife, weak rulers, and ambitious provincial governors began to loosen the imperial grip. The once mighty Mauryan state became a patchwork of competing powers. Tax collection became irregular, local rulers asserted autonomy, and the imperial army weakened.

The great highways that connected Pataliputra (modern-day Patna) to distant provinces were no longer patrolled effectively. Trade declined. Political uncertainty began to choke the vibrant economy.

2. Foreign Invasions and Fragmentation

The decline of Mauryan authority created a vacuum. Power abhors a vacuum, and soon, foreign powers stepped in. The Indo-Greeks from the northwest made inroads, followed by Shunga dynasty and Kanva dynasty.

But none could recreate the Mauryan scale. Instead of one empire, the subcontinent splintered into many smaller kingdoms.

Pataliputra, once the nerve center of an empire, began to lose its centrality. The royal court grew weaker. Administrative institutions, once famed for their efficiency, became corrupt and slow.

3. The Shift of Power Away from Magadh

By the 1st century CE, new centers of power were emerging outside Bihar. The Kushan Empire, with its capital in the northwest, dominated trade and politics. Later, the Gupta Empire revived some of Bihar's glory—especially under Chandragupta I and Samudragupta—but the heart of the Gupta Empire lay slightly westward, around present-day Uttar Pradesh.

Bihar still produced scholars, monks, and ideas, but it was no longer the epicenter. Power had shifted. Trade routes began favoring western India and the Deccan. Ports along the western coast became gateways to the world. Bihar, once at the crossroads of empires, became a quieter, more provincial region.

4. The Fading of Nalanda and Vikramshila

Nalanda University and Vikramshila University stood as proud symbols of Bihar's intellectual might.

For centuries, scholars from Tibet, China, Korea, and Southeast Asia traveled to study there. Debates on logic, mathematics, metaphysics, and medicine filled their courtyards.

But by the 10th century CE, even these luminous centers began to fade. Patronage from kings grew uncertain as local rulers faced wars and invasions. The rich monastic endowments were no longer replenished.

Students dwindled. Buildings, once alive with chants and discussions, began to fall silent. A few dedicated monks kept the flame burning, but without political and economic backing, even the greatest universities cannot survive.

5. The Invasion of Bakhtiyar Khilji

The decline reached its tragic climax in the early 13th century. In 1193 CE, Bakhtiyar Khilji, a general of the Turkic army, invaded Bihar. Nalanda and Vikramshila, both unfortified centers of learning, became easy targets.

The libraries, containing hundreds of thousands of manuscripts, were set on fire. Chroniclers wrote that the manuscripts burned for months. It was not just a university that perished, but centuries of accumulated wisdom.

This invasion was not the beginning of decline—it was the final blow to a civilization already weakened by centuries of fragmentation, neglect, and shifting political fortunes.

6. Economic Decline and Collapse of Trade

Ancient Bihar's prosperity had been tied to its fertile soil and strategic location on the Ganga. But as political stability eroded, so did trade. Merchants preferred safer routes.

Canals and irrigation systems built during Mauryan and Gupta times fell into disrepair. Agriculture became less productive. Artisans, who once made Bihar famous for its textiles, pottery, and metalwork, saw their markets disappear.

The decline was not just political—it was social and economic. Poverty deepened. The grandeur of Pataliputra faded into memory.

7. Cultural Survival Amid Political Fall

And yet, despite everything, Bihar's culture did not vanish. The chants of monks echoed in smaller monasteries. Jain and Buddhist pilgrims still visited Bodh Gaya. Folk traditions continued to thrive in villages.

Even when Nalanda was in ruins, monks carried its manuscripts to Tibet and China, ensuring the survival of many teachings. Local crafts, songs, and rituals adapted to changing rulers. Bihar's spirit endured, even if its empire did not.

8. Why Civilizations Decline

Historians often debate why ancient Bihar declined. The reasons are complex:

Overcentralization during Mauryan times made the empire fragile without a strong ruler.

Shifting trade routes reduced Bihar's economic significance.

Invasions and political fragmentation accelerated the fall.

Neglect of infrastructure and learning centers weakened society's foundations.

But perhaps the deeper cause was a failure to adapt to changing times. While other regions rose with new maritime trade or new political formations, ancient Bihar clung to its past glory.

9. A New Era Beckons

The decline of ancient Bihar did not mean the end of Bihar. The region would soon enter a new chapter—with the rise of medieval powers, Turk-Afghan conquests, Mughal rule, and eventually, the colonial era.

What had been an imperial capital would now become a contested frontier—a place where ideas, cultures, and armies collided. The ancient age of emperors and scholars was over. The age of sultans and conquerors was about to begin.

Epilogue to the Chapter

The story of Bihar's ancient decline is not one of defeat but of transition. Empires rise and fall, but civilizations adapt. Even in ruin, Nalanda inspired universities across Asia. Even in decline, the Ganga plains remained fertile and alive.

Bihar lost its throne, but it did not lose its soul.

Chapter 6: Medieval Bihar — Conquests and Change

The embers of ancient Bihar were still warm when a new storm swept across the Gangetic plains. Once the imperial seat of Mauryan and Gupta power, Bihar now stood at the crossroads of invading armies, ambitious sultans, and emerging powers.

Medieval Bihar was not just an era of political change; it was a period when empires rose and fell over its soil, when monasteries turned to ruins, and when new languages, cultures, and religions mingled with the old.

1. The Fall of the Ancient World

By the end of the 12th century CE, Bihar had lost its ancient political autonomy. The devastating invasion of Bakhtiyar Khilji in 1193 CE did more than burn the great libraries of Nalanda University and Vikramshila University — it marked the symbolic end of ancient Bihar.

The once glorious seat of learning became a war-ravaged province. The Buddhist monks who had preserved wisdom for centuries scattered. Bihar was no longer the center; it had become a frontier.

2. The Arrival of the Delhi Sultanate

Bakhtiyar Khilji was a military commander serving under Delhi Sultanate. His conquest of Bihar brought the region firmly under the Sultanate's expanding control.

The Delhi Sultans understood Bihar's strategic importance — fertile lands, a key link to Bengal, and control over the Ganga plains. Pataliputra (now Patna) declined in political importance, while towns like Bihar Sharif and Gaya became administrative and military outposts.

The administration shifted from ancient forms of self-rule and monastic patronage to centralized military governance. The jizya tax was introduced for non-Muslims. Land revenue became the backbone of state income.

3. Resistance and Local Powers

Foreign rule did not go unchallenged. Local Rajput chiefs and other indigenous rulers resisted the Turkic armies. Rebellions flared across the countryside.

Many of these uprisings were not large empires but localized resistance movements — zamindars and chieftains defending their ancestral lands. Though most were crushed, they kept alive a sense of local autonomy and cultural continuity.

4. The Afghan Interlude and Bengal's Shadow

By the 14th and 15th centuries, the power of the Delhi Sultanate began to weaken. Afghan rulers, including the Sur dynasty, began asserting their dominance.

Bihar often fell under the shadow of Bengal's rulers. The Bengal Sultanate controlled large parts of eastern Bihar. This period saw a fusion of Indo-Islamic culture: Persian became the language of administration, while local dialects like Magahi, Bhojpuri, and Maithili continued to thrive among the masses.

Sufi saints and scholars traveled to Bihar during this period, setting up khanqahs (Sufi hospices) that became centers of spiritual and social interaction. Islam spread not by force alone but also through these networks of devotion and dialogue.

5. Sher Shah Suri — Bihar's Afghan Emperor

Sher Shah Suri, one of the most remarkable rulers of medieval India, emerged from Bihar itself. Born as Farid Khan in Sasaram, Sher Shah rose from being a jagirdar to overthrowing the Mughal emperor Humayun and establishing the Sur Empire in 1540 CE.

Sher Shah ruled from Sasaram and Delhi, but his heart remained in Bihar. He reformed the administration, currency, and postal system, and built the Grand Trunk Road, connecting Bengal to the northwest — with Bihar as a crucial artery.

He introduced efficient land revenue systems and made the state more accountable. Even later Mughal rulers admired and adopted his administrative innovations.

Sher Shah's reign was short (he died in 1545 CE), but his impact was monumental. He was perhaps the only medieval ruler who brought Bihar back to the center of imperial politics — if only for a brief time.

6. The Mughal Period — Bihar as a Province

After Sher Shah's death, the Mughal Empire under Akbar regained control of Bihar in 1576. For the next two centuries, Bihar remained a province under Mughal rule.

Unlike the Delhi Sultanate, the Mughal administration was more systematic. Land revenue was carefully assessed, irrigation projects were revived, and Patna grew into a thriving urban center.

Patna became famous for its saltpetre production, an essential ingredient in gunpowder. European traders — Portuguese, Dutch, French, and English — began arriving by river, turning Bihar into a hub of global trade.

But Mughal rule also meant integration into a larger imperial system, which limited Bihar's political independence. Local elites became part of the Mughal bureaucracy, while villages continued their traditional life.

7. Cultural and Religious Transformation

Medieval Bihar saw layers of cultures intertwining:

Buddhist and Hindu traditions persisted in temples and folk rituals.

Sufi shrines became spaces of syncretic worship.

Persian, Urdu, and local languages coexisted.

Fairs and festivals like Chhath, which originated in Bihar, continued to thrive. Even under foreign rule, Bihar's cultural core adapted rather than disappeared.

Important Sufi centers emerged in places like Bihar Sharif and Maner Sharif, where saints like Makhdoom Yahya Maneri became revered figures across communities.

8. Economic Changes and Social Stratification

While agriculture remained the backbone of the economy, new patterns of land control emerged. Zamindars collected revenue for the state and often exploited peasants. This strengthened landlordism, which would later shape Bihar's colonial and modern politics.

Urban centers like Patna prospered through trade in textiles, opium, saltpetre, and indigo. Yet, the benefits rarely reached the rural masses. Bihar was part of the empire's wealth extraction system, its surplus flowing to Delhi and beyond.

9. The Decline of the Mughals and the Rise of the British

By the early 18th century, the Mughal Empire began to crumble under the weight of internal strife and regional rebellions. In this power vacuum, new actors entered the scene — most notably, the British East India Company.

European traders had already set up factories along the Ganga. When the Mughal grip loosened, they saw their chance to expand. The Battle of Buxar in 1764, fought not far from Patna, would mark the beginning of colonial control over Bihar — but that belongs to the next chapter.

10. Medieval Bihar: A Bridge Between Ages

Medieval Bihar was not an age of darkness, as colonial historians once claimed. It was a bridge between the ancient and modern — a time of conquest, yes, but also of cultural exchange, spiritual synthesis, and economic reorientation.

It was during this era that:

Bihar connected the Persian-Islamic world with the Indic-Buddhist past.

New languages, foods, music, and architecture blended.

Political power left Bihar's hands, but cultural identity deepened.

Epilogue to the Chapter

The medieval period turned Bihar from an imperial core into a frontier province, yet it also planted seeds that would shape its future: landlordism, linguistic diversity, cultural fusion, and strategic importance in trade.

As the Mughal empire weakened, the Ganga once again became a corridor of change — but this time, the sails belonged to European ships.

Bihar was about to enter a new and turbulent chapter: the colonial era, where its fields and people would fuel an empire an ocean away.

Chapter 7: Bihar in the Freedom Struggle — The Land that Stirred a Nation

The 19th and early 20th centuries marked a dramatic new era in Bihar's history. After centuries of being ruled by distant powers — Turkic, Mughal, and British — the people of Bihar began to rise with a new sense of purpose. This wasn't the resistance of zamindars or local rajas anymore. It was the awakening of a people, the stirring of farmers, students, women, and workers who together became part of one of the greatest mass movements in human history: India's freedom struggle.

Bihar may not have always been at the center of Delhi's politics, but during the independence movement, its soil became a battlefield of ideas and courage. From the indigo fields of Champaran to the jails of Patna, from revolutionary hideouts to Congress meetings, Bihar's people wrote their own bold chapter in the story of freedom.

1. Colonial Bihar: Seeds of Discontent

When the British East India Company defeated the Mughal forces and their allies in the Battle of Buxar (1764), Bihar officially came under British control. Over the next century, colonial rule reshaped the region's economy and society in ways both brutal and lasting.

The Permanent Settlement of 1793 created a class of powerful zamindars who acted as intermediaries between the British and the peasantry. This system squeezed the farmers — the real backbone of Bihar —

to their limits. Taxes were fixed and often harsh; famines became frequent; traditional industries such as weaving and pottery declined.

British exploitation was not only economic. It was also cultural. Bihar, once a land of universities, found its education system hollowed out. English replaced Persian as the language of administration, and indigenous schools were neglected. Yet, beneath this oppression, the spark of resistance was slowly kindling.

2. The First War of Independence — 1857

The Indian Rebellion of 1857 — called the Sepoy Mutiny by the British and the First War of Independence by Indian nationalists — was the first major eruption against colonial rule. Bihar played a crucial role in this uprising.

In the district of Jagdishpur, a legendary figure rose to challenge the British: Kunwar Singh. At nearly 80 years old, this zamindar-turned-revolutionary led a formidable rebellion. A skilled tactician, Kunwar Singh outwitted British forces multiple times. Even after losing one hand in battle, he continued to fight — a symbol of undying courage.

Though the rebellion was ultimately suppressed, Kunwar Singh became a folk hero, inspiring generations of Biharis. His struggle showed that the spirit of resistance in Bihar was not passive but fierce.

3. Rise of New Nationalism — Late 19th Century

After the 1857 rebellion, the British cracked down hard. But they could not crush the growing national consciousness. Western education — ironically introduced by the British — also gave rise to a new class of lawyers, teachers, and students who began questioning colonial rule.

In Patna, Muzaffarpur, and Bhagalpur, literary societies and political groups emerged. Newspapers in Hindi, Urdu, and English began discussing nationalism. The early political movement in Bihar was linked to the broader currents of the Indian National Congress, formed in 1885.

Figures like Sachchidananda Sinha and Rajendra Prasad were part of this new educated elite who would later become pillars of the independence movement.

4. The Indigo Fields of Champaran — 1917

Champaran Satyagraha was the turning point — not just for Bihar but for India's freedom movement. In 1917, peasants in Champaran, in north Bihar, suffered under the oppressive "tinkathia" system. British planters forced them to grow indigo on a portion of their land and sell it at fixed low prices, leaving them in debt and misery.

When local leaders like Raj Kumar Shukla appealed for help, Mahatma Gandhi decided to visit Champaran. It was Gandhi's first major satyagraha in India. The movement was extraordinary. Gandhi did not arrive with an army or weapons. He came with the power of nonviolent resistance. He listened to peasants, mobilized lawyers and students, and organized mass protests. When ordered to leave by the British, Gandhi refused — asserting the moral right of Indians to stand up against injustice.

The Champaran Satyagraha forced the British to appoint an inquiry committee and eventually reform the tinkathia system. More importantly, it catapulted Gandhi into national leadership and gave Bihar a permanent place in the story of Indian independence.

5. Rajendra Prasad — The Scholar of the Struggle

Among those who worked closely with Gandhi in Champaran was a quiet, deeply principled lawyer from Bihar: Rajendra Prasad.

Born in Siwan, Prasad was a brilliant student who could have chosen a comfortable life. Instead, he became one of Gandhi's closest allies. He left his legal career to serve the national movement full-time. He organized relief during floods, led the Bihar Congress, and inspired thousands of young Biharis.

Rajendra Prasad's journey mirrors Bihar's role in the freedom struggle — intellectual clarity combined with grassroots activism. He would later become independent India's first President, but his foundation was laid in the dusty villages of Champaran.

6. Revolutionary Currents — Beyond Nonviolence

While Gandhi's nonviolent movement was dominant, Bihar also had its share of revolutionaries who believed in armed resistance. Cities like Patna and Muzaffarpur became centers of underground networks.

In 1908, Khudiram Bose — though from Bengal — carried out a bombing in Muzaffarpur targeting British magistrate Kingsford. He was captured and executed, but his martyrdom inspired many Bihari youth. Secret groups distributed pamphlets, smuggled weapons, and plotted acts of defiance.

This shows Bihar's movement was not one-dimensional — it was a tapestry of ideologies united by the common goal of ending British rule.

7. The Non-Cooperation and Civil Disobedience Movements

When Gandhi launched the Non-Cooperation Movement in 1920, Bihar responded with enthusiasm. Students boycotted government schools. Lawyers gave up their practice. Khadi spinning and village industries gained momentum.

During the Civil Disobedience Movement of the 1930s, salt satyagrahas, protests, and jail bharo campaigns spread across Bihar. Rural women participated in large numbers, often for the first time in political history. Their courage shook colonial confidence.

8. The Quit India Movement — 1942

When the Quit India Movement was announced in August 1942, Bihar became one of the most volatile regions. Students and peasants organized mass demonstrations, attacks on communication lines, and strikes.

Patna and other districts witnessed fierce confrontations with colonial forces. The Patna Secretariat bombing and train disruptions became legendary acts of resistance. Though brutally suppressed, this movement showed the mass politicization of Bihar — from cities to the remotest villages.

9. Women in the Struggle

Bihar's freedom movement was not just led by men. Women like Annie Besant's supporters, Rajkumari Amrit Kaur (though from outside), and Bihari activists such as Phulena Prasad's contemporaries inspired local women to step out.

They joined pickets, protests, and underground movements. In rural Bihar, women smuggled messages, organized food for satyagrahis, and kept the movement alive when leaders were jailed.

10. The Final March — 1946 to Independence

As independence neared, Bihar continued to be politically active. The 1946 elections saw the Indian National Congress winning overwhelming support. But the province also faced communal tensions, as in many parts of India, leading to tragic violence in some areas.

Bihar's leaders played key roles in negotiating the shape of a new India. Rajendra Prasad became the President of the Constituent Assembly. Bihari voices were present in the debates that crafted the Constitution.

On August 15, 1947, when the tricolor was raised, Bihar stood as a proud contributor to India's freedom, not as a bystander.

11. Legacy of Bihar in the Freedom Struggle

Bihar's contribution to the independence movement was unique:

It gave India Champaran, the movement that defined Gandhi's leadership.

It produced leaders like Rajendra Prasad, who shaped the nation's democratic institutions.

It kept alive folk resistance, making the movement not just elite but deeply rooted in villages.

It combined nonviolence and revolution, showing the diversity of the struggle.

12. The Dawn of a New Era

Independence was not the end of Bihar's story. In many ways, it was the beginning of a new struggle — to build a just, equitable society. The colonial chains were broken, but the legacies of zamindari, poverty, and migration would remain challenges.

Yet, the memory of Champaran, Kunwar Singh, and countless unnamed heroes continued to inspire generations. Bihar may have been economically poor, but it was politically rich — a nursery of revolutionaries, freedom fighters, and thinkers.

Epilogue to the Chapter

Bihar's role in the freedom struggle is not just a regional footnote. It is a central pillar in India's journey to independence. Its fields became the stage of satyagraha, its people became symbols of resilience, and its leaders helped shape the destiny of a new nation.

As the sun rose on independent India, the same soil that had once seen the rise of Ashoka and the fall of empires now witnessed the birth of a democratic republic.

Chapter 8: Women and Reformers of Bihar

For centuries, the history of Bihar has often been told through the stories of kings, conquerors, and political movements. But beneath the surface, quiet revolutions were unfolding—led by women who defied expectations and reformers who dared to dream of a better society. Their actions may not always have made it to the headlines of their time, but they shaped the character of Bihar as profoundly as emperors and politicians did.

1. Women in Ancient and Medieval Bihar

In ancient Bihar, especially during the Mauryan and Gupta periods, women enjoyed a relatively higher status compared to later centuries. Historical sources and Buddhist texts indicate that women could become scholars, poets, and spiritual leaders.

One of the earliest known women associated with Bihar's spiritual history is Bhadda Kapilani, a contemporary of the Buddha. She was one of the first women to join the Buddhist Sangha, symbolizing the inclusive spiritual culture of Magadh.

But over time, particularly during the medieval period, women's roles became more confined. The patriarchal structures of both feudal and religious systems restricted their education and mobility. Yet even in these restrictive times, women resisted—not always through rebellion, but through resilience.

2. Women in Folk Traditions and Rural Resistance

Bihar's villages have long been nurseries of powerful women. Folk songs, oral epics, and local legends tell stories of women who led communities during floods, famines, or wars.

Figures like Sita Mai—an idealized version of Sita, who is believed in local folklore to have been born in Sitamarhi—became symbols of strength, not submission. While mythology presented her as a figure of devotion, folk traditions elevated her as a woman of will and resilience.

Women also played key roles in preserving cultural heritage—through festivals, songs (sohar, jorana, chhath geet), and rituals like Chhath Puja. In times when formal political power excluded them, they found strength in cultural power.

3. The Dawn of Modern Reform Movements

The 19th and early 20th centuries brought winds of change. The spread of Western education, the influence of reformist movements, and the early nationalist struggle created space for new conversations on women's rights and social reform.

Bihar saw the rise of remarkable reformers—men and women—who challenged orthodox practices like child marriage, untouchability, and gender discrimination.

One of the most influential reformers was Swami Sahajanand Saraswati, who, while known for his peasant movements, also spoke about the dignity of marginalized communities, including women.

Others, like Rajendra Prasad and Anugrah Narayan Sinha, supported education and women's participation in nationalist activities.

4. The Pioneer: Rajkumari Devi (Kisan Chachi)

Rajkumari Devi, affectionately known as Kisan Chachi, emerged from rural Muzaffarpur as a symbol of what rural women could achieve when given opportunities. A small-scale farmer, she turned her knowledge of organic farming into a cooperative model that empowered other women.

Through agriculture, she challenged gender norms and inspired thousands. Her recognition with national awards in later years was not just personal achievement—it represented a shift in how society viewed rural women.

5. The Freedom Struggle: Women in Action

During India's freedom struggle, Bihar became a hotbed of revolutionary activity. Women were not passive observers—they were on the frontlines.

Rajkumari Gupta and other unsung heroines worked as couriers, intelligence gatherers, and fundraisers for underground movements.

Usha Mehta, though not from Bihar, inspired many young women activists in the region.

Women participated in protests, faced lathi charges, and went to jail alongside their male counterparts.

Quit India Movement of 1942 saw women from small towns and villages take to the streets. Their courage did not always make the headlines, but it strengthened the backbone of the movement.

6. Social Reformers and Education Pioneers

The post-independence era saw education become a powerful tool for women's empowerment. Reformers worked to establish girls' schools and hostels, often facing fierce opposition.

Phulrenu Guha played a key role in promoting women's education and social justice in the region.

Ram Lakhan Singh Yadav and others worked to expand educational infrastructure in rural Bihar.

Missionary schools and state initiatives slowly began to create educational opportunities for girls, though progress remained uneven.

Education gave birth to a new generation of female teachers, nurses, social workers, and activists who would shape Bihar's social landscape in the late 20th century.

7. Jayaprakash Narayan and the Politics of People

Jayaprakash Narayan, the great socialist leader, had a profound impact on Bihar's reform movements. His Total Revolution campaign in the 1970s encouraged youth, women, and marginalized communities to actively participate in politics and social change.

Women were no longer just beneficiaries of reform—they became leaders of it. Many who were inspired by JP's movement later entered politics, civil society, and grassroots activism.

8. Women in Modern Bihar: Breaking New Barriers

The late 20th and early 21st centuries saw women from Bihar emerge as powerful figures in politics, activism, and public life.

Rabri Devi became the first woman Chief Minister of Bihar in 1997—a symbolic moment, regardless of political opinions.

Arunima Sinha, though not born in Bihar but inspiring many in the state, broke physical barriers as a mountaineer.

Grassroots leaders, self-help group members, and panchayat representatives transformed village governance through reservation policies for women.

Schemes promoting girls' education and women's self-help groups created new avenues for empowerment. Women who once were silent participants in rural society became decision-makers.

9. Reformers Beyond Gender: A Broader Vision

Bihar's reformers were not limited to women's issues—they sought to reshape society itself.

Baba Nagarjun and Ramdhari Singh Dinkar used poetry to challenge oppression.

Swami Sahajanand Saraswati mobilized peasants against feudal exploitation.

Jayaprakash Narayan envisioned a democracy rooted in justice and equality.

Their work indirectly opened doors for women by challenging the very structures that marginalized them.

10. Cultural Icons and the Power of Representation

Art, cinema, and literature have been powerful platforms for women's voices. Female characters in Maithili and Bhojpuri literature often reflected social realities—sometimes idealized, sometimes rebellious.

In contemporary times, Bihari women have made their mark in cinema, literature, civil services, and activism. Their stories represent a slow but irreversible shift—from the margins to the mainstream.

11. Challenges That Remain

While Bihar has made strides in women's empowerment, challenges remain.

Literacy rates among women still lag behind the national average.

Economic empowerment is limited in many rural areas.

Early marriage and patriarchal customs persist.

Political participation sometimes remains symbolic rather than substantive.

But these challenges do not overshadow the progress. They are reminders of the work still to be done.

12. The Torchbearers of Tomorrow

Today's young women in Bihar stand on the shoulders of generations who fought quietly but fiercely for dignity. Their stories are not just about empowerment—they are about transformation.

From the farmers' fields of Muzaffarpur to the debating halls of Patna, from panchayat meetings to UPSC examinations, Bihari women are rewriting their narrative. Reformers—both male and female—continue to work in health, education, law, and rights movements, keeping the spirit of change alive.

Epilogue to the Chapter

The story of Bihar cannot be told without the story of its women and reformers. They are the silent architects of the state's modern identity. Their courage is not always found in battlefields or assemblies, but in classrooms, kitchens, farms, and village squares.

Empires rose and fell, political leaders came and went, but the resilience of Bihar's women—and the reformers who supported them—remains one of the state's most enduring legacies.

Chapter 9: Bhumihars — History, Influence, Politics, and Modern Identity

In the complex tapestry of caste, class, and politics in North India—especially in Bihar, eastern Uttar Pradesh, and adjoining regions—the Bhumihar community occupies a rather fascinating and at times paradoxical position. Traditionally landholders claiming Brahmin status, with roots in agrarian power and political mobilization, the Bhumihars have been both agents and subjects of social change. Their evolution over time—from landowning elite to contested caste actors negotiating identity and power—reflects larger shifts in Indian society: colonial land regimes, post-independence reform, caste mobilizations, and the ascendancy of new political identities.

In this chapter, we trace the historical origins and claims of the Bhumihars; explore their socio-economic base and influence under colonial and postcolonial regimes; investigate their political trajectory and conflicts of the late 20th century; and critically examine how Bhumihars are reimagining their identity in contemporary India—balancing tradition, modernity, and politics.

Historical Origins and Self-Interpretation

Etymology and early claims

The term "Bhumihar" is relatively late in historical record, found in official documents as early as 1865 in the records of the United Provinces. It comes from bhūmi ("land") combined with hār (one who holds), signaling their identity as landholders. Some sources also render it as Bhumihar Brahmin, emphasizing the community's aspiration to Brahmin status. The older colloquial name Babhan (or Bābhān) is often treated as an Apabhramsha (distorted) form of "Brahman."

Rather than claiming descent from ancient rishis in the same way other Brahmin lineages do, many Bhumihars narrated a mythic identity tied to Parashurama, the warrior-Brahmin avatar of Vishnu, who is traditionally said to have destroyed Kshatriyas and re-established Brahmin dominance. Some versions claim that, in the aftermath, these Brahmins were granted lands and became agriculturists, blending priesthood and landholding. Within caste association literature, this dual identity—warrior + Brahmin, warrior through landholding—is pivotal in how Bhumihars project themselves today.

Another narrative positions Bhumihars as essentially secular Brahmins: Brahmins who held grants of land (for performance of secular or administrative functions) instead of performing full priestly duties. In that sense, any Brahmin holding a secular fief or land grant became Bhumihar in function. This helps explain why Bhumihars historically have, unlike many Brahmins, engaged in agriculture and even martial roles rather than exclusively in ritual priestly functions.

Thus, from early on, Bhumihars fashioned an identity that combined ritual prestige (Brahmin) with material dominion (land). But their claim to Brahmin status has never been unchallenged. Other Brahmin groups have sometimes resisted Bhumihar inclusion in the Brahmin fold, seeing them as a heterodox or hybrid group.

Land, feudal power, and princely holdings

By the eighteenth and nineteenth centuries, especially in Bihar and eastern Uttar Pradesh, many Bhumihars had risen as zamindars and feudal landlords. They controlled large tracts of agricultural land, wielded social influence over tenant cultivators (often from lower castes), and sometimes commanded private militias to enforce their economic dominance.

Some Bhumihar families also rose to princely or semi-princely status. For example, the Tekari Raj in Gaya (South Bihar) was controlled by a Bhumihar family, and there were smaller estates and jagirs in regions such as Bettiah, Sheohar, Hathwa, Tamukhi, and others. These holdings conferred not just wealth but also political and judicial authority over large rural hinterlands.

In this feudal configuration, the Bhumihars often played dual roles: as landlords extracting surplus and maintaining control, and as ritual elites asserting moral legitimacy. Their dual identity allowed them to combine agrarian dominance with Brahminical symbolisms—supporting temples, sponsoring religious institutions, and shaping local ritual culture.

Colonial and Early Postcolonial Transitions

Colonial land reforms and the challenge to dominance
The British colonial regime introduced legal changes—

land settlement, codification of rights, and abolition or weakening of some traditional feudal rights—that gradually challenged older agrarian relations. Although in many places, upper-caste landlords (including Bhumihars) adapted by consolidating holdings or renting lands, the transformation altered the balance between landlords and cultivators.

More significantly, the early post-independence land reform policies—ceiling laws, tenancy reforms, and abolition of intermediaries—aimed to dismantle the landlord-based structure. In Bihar, though land reforms were often weakly enforced, they did create new classes of occupancy tenants who staked claims to land, and new agrarian classes less dependent on landlord patronage.

Because Bhumihars were a relatively small community (about 2.9% in 1931, though their spatial presence and influence was greater) and yet held disproportionate land power, these reforms forced them to adapt politically. They began to form caste associations, promote education, and cultivate non-agrarian professions to retain social relevance.

Early political entry

From the 1930s onwards, individuals from the Bhumihar community entered modern politics and bureaucracy. They used their resources, education, and prestige to compete for elected offices. Bihar's early leaders included Bhumihars. For instance, Sri Krishna Sinha, a Bhumihar, became the first Chief Minister of Bihar (1946 onward in interim governments, and post independence). The community also lent prominent names to Congress and other political formations.

Between 1952 and 1962, the four upper-caste castes—Brahmins, Rajputs, Bhumihars, and Kayasthas—dominated Congress representation in Bihar, commanding over 40% of Congress MLAs. This reveals how the older caste elite (including Bhumihars) held sway in electoral politics for at least the initial decades of independent India before the assertion of backward-caste alliances.

Thus, the Bhumihars combined land-derived caste dominance with modern political strategy in the early decades of electoral democracy.

Political Clout, Conflict, and Transformation

The dominance phase and resistance

From the 1960s into the 1980s, Bhumihars remained among the dominant castes in Bihar, but their dominance was contested more forcefully as backward caste mobilization gained momentum. As Indian politics shifted from elite control to mass mobilization, caste groups previously marginalized by the old order pushed back.

In this period, caste violence became a key instrument of social assertion. Bhumihars, because of their landholding dominance and caste status, were often involved (as perpetrators or victims) in violent clashes with lower castes or leftist mobilization. The logic was often: if symbolic dominance is being challenged, physical force might reassert territorially rooted power.

One particularly notorious example was the Bathani Tola massacre (1996), in which a Bhumihar militia group, Ranvir Sena, attacked Dalit laborers in Bhojpur district in response to demands for higher wages. Similarly, in Bara massacre (1992), Maoist forces attacked Bhumihar men in Gaya district, killing dozens in retaliation for earlier upper-caste violence. The Raghopur massacre (1997) was another incident where Naxalites targeted Bhumihars.

These violent events were not anomalies but emblematic of deeper structural tensions: land inequality, caste hierarchies, and mobilization of marginalized groups. Bhumihars were defending (or reviving) a declining agrarian supremacy in the face of rising lower-caste assertion.

Academic studies note a shift in tactics over time—from direct physical violence to symbolic violence (e.g., through rituals, exclusion, caste associations, control of cultural capital). As caste conflicts became more constrained legally and morally, Bhumihars increasingly leaned on cultural and ideological assertion—claiming ritual primacy, aligning with Hindutva, forging caste associations—to maintain status.

Political realignments and electoral competition

By the 1990s, the politics of Bihar underwent a profound transformation. The rise of Lalu Prasad Yadav and the assertion of Backward Castes (OBCs)—Yadavs, Kurmis, and others—reshaped electoral coalitions and challenged upper caste dominance. In this new landscape, Bhumihars had to reposition.

Some segments of the community gravitated toward Hindutva politics, seeing an alliance with the Bharatiya Janata Party and other right-wing forces as a way to retain symbolic dominance in a shifting social order. Others attempted to build caste solidarity, caste federations, and educational institutions to maintain internal cohesion.

Yet, because they were numerically small, Bhumihars had to operate often as "linchpin castes"—groups whose allegiance could tip electoral outcomes in key constituencies. Their political value was magnified in multi-caste electoral arithmetic.

In some cases, Bhumihars allied with upper backward castes or even with "upper castes" like Rajputs and Brahmins to counterbalance OBC dominance. The politics became less about pure superordinate caste identity and more about electoral calculation, coalition building, and survival.

The politics of memory and initiative

One notable domain of political intervention for Bhumihars has been caste associations and community institutions. These organizations promote community-specific welfare (scholarships, schools, member networks), cultural rituals, and political lobbying. Over decades, the Bhumihar caste associations have grown more sophisticated, with internal hierarchies, publications, youth wings, and electoral strategies.

By institutionalizing caste identity, Bhumihars have sought to reproduce social cohesion, guard against demographic decline, and buffer against political marginalization. This associational activism also helps the community package itself as a "respectable" caste identity amid a climate where purely elitist caste claims face critique.

Modern Identity, Challenges, and Reimaginings

Social change, migration, and occupational shifts

In recent decades, many Bhumihar families are moving away from dependence on landholdings alone. Economic pressures, fragmentation of land, and diminishing returns from agriculture have pushed younger generations into migration, salaried services, teaching, bureaucracy, and business. As a result, the link between caste identity and agrarian dominance is becoming attenuated for many.

Among women in Bhumihar households, researchers find nuanced negotiations of caste norms. "Left-behind" Bhumihar women in villages (whose men have migrated) still abide by many caste-gender codes but reinterpret them through new frameworks of agency, mobility, and aspiration.

Thus, modern Bhumihars are more heterogeneous: some remain large landholders, others small farmers, yet others are urban professionals distancing themselves from caste-based agrarian politics.

Identity discourse, status negotiation, and Hindutva alignment

Because the Bhumihar claim to Brahminical status has always been somewhat contested, much of contemporary identity-building is about status legitimization—ritual, symbolic, and cultural. Caste associations and intellectuals produce discourses emphasizing the "warrior Brahmin" origins, moral purity, and ritual correctness.

In the late 20th and early 21st centuries, many Bhumihars have gravitated toward Hindutva politics. By aligning with a pan-Hindu political identity, they attempt both to transcend narrower caste-based divisions and to recycle their caste prestige into broader religious symbolism. This alignment also offers political leverage: in multi-caste Hindu electorates, sectarian solidarity can sometimes override local antagonisms.

But this alignment is not unproblematic—some younger Bhumihars quietly question the narrowness of caste-based politics, are drawn to liberal education, or wish to transcend identity. Thus, the community today encompasses tension between tradition and modernity, insiders and reformers.

Challenges: demographic limits and social transformation

One structural challenge is the numerical limitation of the community. In states like Bihar, Bhumihars are a small minority. With the rise of large OBC and Dalit coalitions, their ability to dominate electorally is constrained. Their influence now depends more on strategic presence (in key constituencies, or in bureaucracy) rather than mass dominance.

Second, the changing land regime—fragmentation, commercialization, land ceiling laws, agricultural distress—attenuates traditional landlord power. As more people sell land or shift to non-farm incomes, the agrarian basis of caste dominance weakens.

Third, legal and moral norms around caste violence have made overt coercion riskier politically. The Bhumihar community thus increasingly depends on soft power, cultural capital, educational status, and network mobilization rather than sheer brute force.

Fourth, generational change means that younger Bhumihars may feel less tied to caste politics or feudal legacy. Some may prefer meritocratic identities or broader social platforms to narrow caste frameworks.

Strategies of adaptation and assertion

To respond to these challenges, Bhumihars are employing multiple strategies:

Educational investment and professionalization: encouraging youth into government services, teaching, engineering, and professional roles. This creates new metrics of prestige beyond landholding.

Institutional consolidation: refining caste associations, publishing academic journals, running scholarship schemes, building alumni networks, and community welfare platforms—thus maintaining internal solidarity and external visibility.

Cultural capital and ritual assertion: sponsorship of temples, festivals, pilgrimages, and symbolic events to anchor ritual status in the public sphere.

Political pragmatism: forging flexible alliances, supporting Hindutva where useful, contesting local seats with coalition math, and acting as kingmakers in tight contests.

Hybrid identity projection: crafting discourse that emphasizes being both Brahmin and warrior (the "warrior-Brahmin" trope), merging tradition with modern roles, and projecting an image of dignified elitism without overt feudalism.

Thus, while their era of hegemonic dominance may have receded, Bhumihars continue to negotiate space in the new social order through adaptive strategies and identity work.

Bhumihars in Contemporary Bihar: Some Vignettes

To ground the theoretical discussion, a few snapshots from Bihar's social and political life illustrate how Bhumihars continue to matter—politically, socially, and symbolically:

In electoral contests, even when not numerically dominant, Bhumihars are sought after in certain assembly segments as swing voters or elite opinion makers. Their endorsement can tilt local alliances.

In memory politics, Bhumihars often highlight illustrious personalities from their community—politicians, social reformers, freedom fighters—to reassert pride and identity.

Conflict memory remains potent: massacres like Bara (1992), Raghopur (1997), or Bathani Tola (1996) are sometimes invoked in community narratives as evidence of suffering or moral victimhood.

Women's voices from within Bhumihar households express the disjunction between caste norms and changing economic realities. Their negotiations with tradition and aspiration reflect inner tensions of caste life.

In villages where Bhumihars remain landholders, they may still carry moral authority, but with diminished coercive power. Younger Bhumihars may be less invested in traditional patron-client relations and more in professional networks.

These vignettes show that Bhumihars are neither relics nor omnipotent elites—but active agents in a changing social order.

Critical Reflections: Power, Identity, and Future Trajectories When considering the Bhumihar trajectory, a few critical reflections emerge.

1. Caste and class entwined: The Bhumihar narrative underscores that caste cannot be understood apart from class. Their dominance emerged from land, their decline correlates with agrarian restructuring, and their strategies now hinge on educational/class mobility.

2. Identity as struggle: The Bhumihar claim to Brahmin status has always entailed internal struggle—symbolic contestation, reinterpretation, and status maintenance. Their journey reveals that caste identity is not a fixed given but a negotiated terrain.

3. Violence and legitimacy: The shift from overt physical coercion to symbolic assertion is notable. In their earlier dominance, violence (or threat thereof) was a tool of control; in the modern era, moral, cultural, and political legitimacy become more critical.

4. Limits of dominance in plural democracy: In a democratic age, small numerical communities, however entrenched, cannot dominate indefinitely. Their continued relevance depends on flexible alliances, institutional embedding, and adaptation to changing social mores.

5. Generational disjuncture: Younger Bhumihars—urban, professional, mobile—may not feel bound by caste-based politics or legacy. The continuity of collective identity may depend on how well institutions can carry past narratives into new contexts.

Conclusion

The story of Bhumihars is not one of static superiority or inevitable decline—but of a community in constant negotiation. From their early identity claims (warrior-Brahmin, landholder-Brahmin) to their feudal power, political dominance, confrontation with lower-caste assertion, and current reinventions, Bhumihars mirror broader currents in Indian society: shifts in agrarian structure, democratization, mass mobilization, and identity politics.

In the twenty-first century, their challenge is to reinvent relevance: not through coercion, but through institutions, narrative, education, and alliance. Whether they succeed in sustaining a dignified place—neither feudal relic nor irrelevant minority—depends on their capacity to evolve.

Chapter 10: The Bifurcation — When Jharkhand Was Born

The state of Bihar has a long, complex history of shifting boundaries, empires, and administrative reorganizations. From the days of the Mauryan Empire to the Mughal era, it has been the political and cultural heartland of eastern India. However, the late 20th century brought the most dramatic change to Bihar's modern political map: the birth of Jharkhand in 2000, which carved out the mineral-rich southern part of the state, forever altering Bihar's geography, economy, and identity.

1. Historical Context: The Roots of Jharkhand

The idea of a separate Jharkhand did not emerge overnight. The region comprising present-day Jharkhand — the Chotanagpur plateau and Santhal Parganas — has been home to indigenous tribal communities for centuries. These communities, including Santhals, Oraons, Mundas, and Ho, maintained distinct languages, cultures, and governance systems.

During British colonial rule, the region was administered as part of Bihar, Orissa, and Bengal at different times, but tribal communities often faced exploitation. Land alienation, forced labor, and mining operations by the British disrupted traditional livelihoods.

Even after independence, southern Bihar continued to face:

Economic neglect compared to the northern plains.

Limited political representation in the state assembly.

Underdevelopment of infrastructure, education, and healthcare.

This historical marginalization planted the seeds for the demand for a separate state.

2. Tribal Movements and Early Agitations

The early tribal uprisings were rooted in resistance to exploitation, often economic rather than political.

The Munda Rebellion (1899–1900), led by Birsa Munda, became legendary. Birsa demanded the restoration of tribal lands and rights and opposed British interference in traditional governance. Though crushed, the rebellion highlighted the distinctiveness and grievances of tribal communities in southern Bihar.

Later movements in the 20th century, such as the Jharkhand Party founded by Jaipal Singh Munda, pushed for a separate state within independent India. The party's demand was clear: tribal identity, culture, and resources should not be submerged under the larger Bihari political structure.

3. Economic Factors and Resource Distribution

Southern Bihar was, and remains, rich in minerals: coal, mica, bauxite, and iron ore. The region's forests and plateaus also provided timber and other resources.

Yet the local population rarely benefited. Wealth generated from mining and industrial activity flowed largely to urban centers in north Bihar, Kolkata, and beyond.

Coal mining in Jharia and Dhanbad became particularly controversial, with labor exploitation and environmental degradation rampant.

Tribal lands were often leased to private companies without local consent.

Economic disparity fueled the argument that a separate state could focus on local development, governance, and resource management, rather than being overshadowed by the politics of northern Bihar.

4. Political Mobilization and Identity Assertion

Post-independence India saw multiple efforts to create Jharkhand.

The Jharkhand Party, active from the 1950s to the 1970s, mobilized tribal communities across southern Bihar. Its demands included land reform, tribal autonomy, and political representation.

Language, culture, and identity became central to the movement. Tribal festivals, folk music, and languages such as Mundari, Santhali, and Ho were promoted as symbols of a distinct Jharkhand identity.

Political alliances shifted over decades. The movement gained traction as regional parties, national parties, and tribal leaders debated the timing, governance, and economic feasibility of a separate state.

5. The Road to Statehood

The path to Jharkhand's creation was long and complex:

1. 1950s–1970s: The Jharkhand Party demanded autonomy but faced resistance from the Bihar government and Congress leadership.

2. 1980s: Regional leaders continued advocacy, emphasizing underdevelopment, displacement, and identity rights.

3. 1990s: Political consensus slowly emerged. National parties recognized that state reorganization could address tribal grievances and stimulate economic development.

The push was aided by broader state reorganization policies in India, which had already created states like Chhattisgarh and Uttarakhand.

6. Birth of Jharkhand: November 15, 2000

Finally, on November 15, 2000, Jharkhand became India's 28th state.

Ranchi became the capital.

Political control shifted to regional leaders from Jharkhand-centric parties.

Bihar's size was reduced, and its population and resource base changed dramatically.

The bifurcation was not just administrative; it was symbolic. It recognized the distinct cultural, economic, and historical identity of the tribal populations in southern Bihar.

Yet, for Bihar, the separation was bittersweet: it lost much of its mineral wealth, including coal-rich Dhanbad and Bokaro steel regions, which would affect economic planning for decades.

7. Social and Economic Impacts on Bihar

The bifurcation had profound effects on Bihar's society and economy:

Loss of Resources: Southern Bihar contributed significantly to the state's GDP through mining and industry. Its separation meant Bihar had to rethink economic strategies, focusing more on agriculture, services, and education.

Political Reorientation: Bihar's politics became concentrated on north Bihar and the Gangetic plains. Leaders had to address agrarian issues, caste dynamics, and urban development more intensively.

Cultural Identity: The creation of Jharkhand also forced Bihar to redefine its identity. For centuries, Bihar had been a single cultural and historical entity; now, it had to cultivate pride in its plains, heritage, and intellectual legacy.

8. Challenges and Opportunities Post-Bifurcation

Post-2000, both Bihar and Jharkhand faced challenges:

For Bihar: Loss of industrial regions required new economic models.

Migration of labor to other states increased.

Infrastructure and governance needed urgent reforms.

For Jharkhand: Managing mineral wealth without exploitation of tribal communities.

Ensuring education, healthcare, and political representation for marginalized populations.

Balancing rapid industrialization with ecological concerns.

Yet the bifurcation also created opportunities:

Bihar could focus on education, agriculture, and urban renewal.

Jharkhand could create development models rooted in tribal identity and resource management.

Both states could now reclaim their cultural heritage and political voices more effectively.

9. Political and Cultural Reflections

The creation of Jharkhand stirred debates about regionalism, identity, and development. Some critics argued it weakened Bihar's economy, while others praised it for recognizing tribal autonomy.

Culturally, the bifurcation highlighted the diversity of eastern India. Bihar retained its historical cities—Patna, Gaya, Nalanda—as intellectual and spiritual hubs, while

Jharkhand focused on tribal culture, natural resources, and ecological heritage.

10. Legacy of the Bifurcation

The bifurcation of Bihar and the creation of Jharkhand is a milestone in Indian federalism. It teaches lessons about:

Balancing ethnic and tribal identity with state governance.

Recognizing historical grievances and economic inequalities.

Using statehood as a tool for development, cultural preservation, and political representation.

It also reshaped Bihar's narrative: no longer a single, massive state, it became smaller but more focused, reclaiming its historical legacy and building a path toward modernization.

Epilogue to the Chapter

The birth of Jharkhand reminds us that boundaries on a map cannot erase culture, history, or aspiration. Bihar may have lost territory, but it retained its soul—the Ganga plains, Nalanda's ruins, and the vibrant life of its people.

Bifurcation was a turning point, marking the end of one administrative era and the beginning of another. It forced both Bihar and Jharkhand to confront their histories, embrace their identities, and plan for futures that reflect both tradition and transformation.

Chapter 11: Post-Independence Bihar

India's independence on August 15, 1947, marked the end of colonial rule, but for Bihar, it was the beginning of a new and complex chapter. The state, with its fertile Gangetic plains, rich history, and vibrant culture, faced the enormous task of rebuilding society, governance, and economy after centuries of political upheaval, colonial exploitation, and economic neglect.

Post-independence Bihar was poised at a crossroads: it had historical prestige, but the challenges of poverty, caste hierarchies, and governance threatened to hold it back. This chapter examines the first five decades of Bihar as part of a free India, highlighting both achievements and struggles.

1. Early Governance and Political Leadership

Bihar's early post-independence politics were dominated by leaders who had played central roles in the freedom movement. The state became a laboratory of democratic governance, balancing national policies with regional needs.

Rajendra Prasad, Bihar's most prominent leader and India's first President, symbolized the state's intellectual and moral capital. His presidency provided Bihar with national recognition and inspired political participation across the state.

Anugrah Narayan Sinha, the first Deputy Chief Minister and Finance Minister, was instrumental in shaping

Bihar's administrative machinery. He focused on revenue reforms, land settlement, and education.

The Indian National Congress dominated politics in these early years, focusing on institution-building, law and order, and rural development. Political participation grew rapidly as the electorate expanded to include millions of newly enfranchised citizens.

2. Land Reforms and Social Change

One of the most pressing challenges was land inequality. Large zamindari estates still controlled vast swathes of fertile land, while peasants and laborers remained marginalized.

The government implemented land reform laws aimed at:

Abolishing the zamindari system.

Redistributing land to small and marginal farmers.

Providing tenancy rights to sharecroppers.

While reforms were enacted on paper, their implementation was patchy due to bureaucratic delays, resistance from powerful landlords, and political compromises. Nevertheless, these reforms laid the groundwork for greater social mobility and the eventual rise of backward caste and Dalit political participation.

3. Economic Challenges and Migration

Bihar faced chronic economic challenges after independence:

Agriculture, though fertile, suffered from outdated methods, irrigation deficits, and poor infrastructure.

Industrialization lagged behind neighboring states, leading to high unemployment.

Floods and environmental degradation periodically devastated crops.

These economic pressures contributed to mass migration, especially to urban centers like Kolkata, Delhi, Mumbai, and even abroad. Bihari laborers became crucial to construction, mining, and industrial sectors elsewhere, giving rise to the enduring "Bihari diaspora" phenomenon.

Migration helped families survive, but it also depleted local talent and slowed Bihar's economic development.

4. Education and Intellectual Revival

Bihar has a proud intellectual tradition, from Nalanda and Vikramshila to modern universities. Post-independence, the state sought to revive its educational legacy:

Institutions like Patna University expanded to provide higher education opportunities.

Technical and medical colleges were established to train professionals.

Literacy campaigns targeted rural areas, though female literacy lagged behind male literacy. Despite these efforts, Bihar struggled with teacher shortages, infrastructural deficits, and political interference, which limited educational outcomes. Yet, the state produced prominent scholars, writers, and administrators, ensuring continuity of its intellectual tradition.

5. Social Movements and Caste Politics

Bihar's society has historically been shaped by caste hierarchies, which influenced land ownership, occupation, and social status. Post-independence, caste politics became a defining feature:

Backward caste movements sought political representation and social justice. Leaders like Karpoori Thakur championed policies favoring backward classes, including reservations in education and employment.

Dalits and marginalized communities began asserting rights, creating new political alignments that challenged traditional elites.

These social movements transformed Bihar from a land dominated by upper castes to a more politically pluralistic society, albeit with tensions and conflicts.

6. Urbanization and Infrastructure Development

Post-independence Bihar witnessed gradual urbanization, especially in Patna, Gaya, Bhagalpur, and Muzaffarpur. The government focused on:

Developing roads, railways, and river transport to improve trade and mobility.

Establishing hospitals, schools, and government offices to enhance public services. Encouraging small-scale industries to diversify the economy.

Despite these efforts, infrastructure development lagged behind demand, and bureaucratic inefficiency and political corruption limited the impact.

7. Political Evolution: 1950s to 1970s

Bihar's post-independence politics reflected national trends and regional dynamics:

Congress dominance continued into the 1960s, though opposition parties began organizing.

Socialist movements, led by leaders like Jayaprakash Narayan, gained traction, advocating for agrarian reform, democracy, and social justice.

These movements created a political culture that emphasized people's participation, protest, and accountability.

Bihar became known as a hotbed of political activism, with grassroots movements shaping state policies.

8. Cultural Revival and Identity

Post-independence Bihar also experienced a cultural revival:

Maithili, Bhojpuri, and Magahi literature flourished.

Folk music, theatre, and festivals were promoted to strengthen regional identity.

Spiritual tourism grew around sites like Bodh Gaya, Rajgir, and Vaishali, connecting Bihar's ancient heritage to modern India.

This cultural revival reaffirmed Bihar's historical significance while integrating it into a modern democratic framework.

9. Challenges in Governance

Despite its potential, Bihar faced persistent governance challenges:

Political instability due to frequent changes in leadership.

Corruption in administration and law enforcement.

Slow implementation of economic and social policies.

These issues limited Bihar's ability to translate its rich resources and talent into sustainable growth, creating structural challenges that would persist for decades.

10. Achievements and Resilience

Despite difficulties, post-independence Bihar achieved significant milestones:

Land reforms reduced feudal power.

Mass education campaigns expanded literacy.

Political activism ensured participation across caste and class lines.

Cultural preservation kept ancient traditions alive while fostering new creative expressions.

The resilience of Bihar's people—farmers, students, workers, and intellectuals—remained a hallmark of its post-independence journey.

11. Bihar in the National Context

Bihar's role in India's post-independence era was disproportionately significant:

It provided leaders at the national level, including the first President, Rajendra Prasad, and influential MPs. Its labor force fueled urban growth across India. Social movements and reform efforts in Bihar influenced policies on caste, labor, and education nationwide. Even as challenges persisted, Bihar retained its identity as a land of ideas, resilience, and historical pride.

12. Looking Ahead

Post-independence Bihar was a state of contrasts:

A rich historical and cultural heritage, A politically active population, And persistent economic and governance challenges. The stage was now set for the late 20th century transformations—including political upheaval, industrial decline, and the eventual rise of new political leaders—which would define Bihar's modern trajectory.

Epilogue to the Chapter

The post-independence era reminds us that freedom alone does not guarantee prosperity. Bihar had achieved political liberation, but the work of economic development, social equality, and governance reform remained. Yet, through all struggles, Bihar continued to produce leaders, thinkers, and social reformers. The seeds planted in this period would later grow intomovements that sought to revive the state's economy, empower its people, and reaffirm its identity.

Chapter 12: The Lalu Era — Jungle Raj and the Criminalization of Politics (1990 – 2005)

In 1990, Bihar entered one of the most turbulent chapters in its modern history. Under the leadership of Lalu Prasad Yadav, the state saw a political and social upheaval unlike any since independence.

Lalu came to power on the promise of "social justice", empowerment of backward classes, and a challenge to the entrenched upper-caste dominance. However, his long tenure became equally known for widespread corruption, criminalization of politics, and a collapse in law and order that gave rise to the phrase "Jungle Raj."

1. The Rise of Lalu Prasad Yadav

In 1990, as part of the Mandal era, Lalu emerged as a charismatic leader of backward classes. His rustic style, powerful oratory, and anti-elite politics won him mass support.

He projected himself as a "messiah of the poor", challenging the traditional elite.

His party — the Rashtriya Janata Dal (RJD) — dominated Bihar's political landscape for 15 years.

However, during this period, governance weakened, and criminal syndicates flourished under political protection.

2. Law and Order Breakdown

From the early 1990s, Bihar experienced an unprecedented spike in violent crimes:

Kidnapping for ransom became a booming "industry."

Armed gangs operated freely, especially in central and north Bihar.

Contract killings, extortion, and political violence grew unchecked.

Many gang leaders either contested elections or had close ties with ruling party figures.

Patna, Muzaffarpur, Siwan, and Begusarai became notorious hotspots for kidnappings. Businessmen, doctors, engineers, and even children of wealthy families were abducted for ransom. Many families sold land or left Bihar altogether for safety.

3. Criminal–Political Nexus

One of the defining features of this era was the merging of crime and politics.

Gang leaders entered politics, winning elections with money and muscle power.

Political leaders protected or allied with criminal gangs to maintain control.

Police and bureaucracy were often pressured to look the other way. A notorious example was the rise of Mohammad Shahabuddin, an RJD MP from Siwan, widely known for his influence and alleged role in organized crime. Shahabuddin's clout was both political and criminal, making Siwan a symbol of Bihar's lawlessness in the late 1990s and early 2000s.

4. High-Profile Criminal Cases

Several high-profile criminal cases during this period shocked the nation and exposed the breakdown of governance:

- **Shilpi Jain murder case (1999)**

A sensational case involving the mysterious death of Shilpi Jain and Gautam Singh. The case, marked by allegations of political cover-ups and interference, became a national symbol of lawlessness in Bihar. It reflected how powerful interests often blocked justice during this period.

- **Kidnapping Industry**

Doctors, engineers, students, and business families were targeted for ransom. According to contemporary reports, hundreds of kidnapping cases went unsolved, and many victims' families fled the state.

- **Crimes Against Women**

Gender-based violence was widespread. Many cases involved intimidation, silence, and impunity, reflecting a climate where women's safety was severely compromised.

5. The Fodder Scam — Corruption at the Top

Perhaps the biggest corruption scandal of the era was the Fodder Scam, a massive financial fraud involving the embezzlement of over ₹900 crore from the state's animal husbandry department.

Fake bills were issued for non-existent fodder and medicines.

Funds meant for cattle welfare were siphoned off through a nexus of politicians, bureaucrats, and suppliers.

Eventually, the scam directly implicated Lalu Prasad Yadav himself, leading to his resignation in 1997.

The fodder scam symbolized systemic corruption and shook public trust in governance.

6. Paper Leaks and "Ghus" Jobs

During this era, recruitment in government jobs was plagued by:

Bribery ("ghus") for postings and promotions.

Paper leaks in competitive exams, leading to widespread distrust among youth.

Political interference in administrative transfers.

For many, getting a government job meant paying bribes or having political connections, undermining merit and morale.

7. Kidnapping and the Exodus of the Middle Class

The kidnapping crisis had long-term socio-economic consequences:

Many industrialists and traders migrated to safer states like Delhi, Gujarat, or Maharashtra.

Private schools, coaching centers, and colleges shut down or relocated.

Investment dried up completely, leaving Bihar economically stagnant.

This "brain drain" and capital flight crippled the state's economic base.

8. Police and Administrative Paralysis

The law-and-order machinery was politicized and demoralized:

Honest officers faced transfers or punishment postings.

Criminals often operated without fear of arrest.

Courts were overburdened, and convictions were rare.

This paralysis created a climate of impunity, where criminals felt untouchable.

9. Media and Public Perception

National media frequently highlighted Bihar as the most lawless state in India. Headlines in the late 1990s and early 2000s often read:

"Kidnapping Capital of India"

"Jungle Raj"

"Where Criminals Rule, Not the State"

Bihar became a symbol of state failure, affecting its reputation for decades.

10. Decline of the Education System

The criminal–political nexus also infiltrated universities and colleges:

Student unions were often controlled by gangs linked to politicians.

Exam malpractices, paper leaks, and violence on campuses were common.

The quality of education plummeted, leading students to migrate out of state.

11. Social Justice vs Governance

Lalu's defenders argued that he empowered backward castes, giving them a voice and political space. Indeed, the upper-caste monopoly on power was broken during this era.

But critics countered that empowerment without governance led to:

Criminalization of politics,

Collapse of institutions, and

Economic stagnation.

Bihar became a cautionary tale: a state where power shifted socially but the rule of law eroded dangerously.

12. Fall of the Regime

By the early 2000s, public anger was mounting:

Infrastructure had crumbled.

Lawlessness was widespread.

Youth saw no future in the state.

The 2005 Assembly elections marked the end of RJD's 15-year rule. The Nitish Kumar–led alliance came to power on the promise of restoring law and order.

Epilogue to the chapter

The Lalu era is remembered with complex emotions in Bihar. It gave a voice to the marginalized, but it also allowed crime, corruption, and chaos to take root.

The state's reputation, economy, and social fabric suffered immensely. Kidnapping, paper leaks, corruption, and criminal–political nexus became national talking points.

This period left deep scars — but also lessons in governance, showing how power without accountability can destroy institutions.

📜 Timeline of Major Criminal and Corruption Incidents (1990–2005)

Year Event / Case Location Nature of Incident Significance

1990 Rise of Lalu Prasad Yadav Bihar (statewide) Political Beginning of RJD rule; promises of "social justice"

1991–1999 Kidnapping wave peaks Patna, Muzaffarpur, Begusarai, Siwan Organized crime Surge in ransom kidnappings of businessmen, doctors, students

1996 Fodder Scam exposed Statewide Corruption (₹900+ crore fraud) One of India's biggest scams; directly implicated Lalu

1997 Resignation of Lalu Prasad Yadav Patna Political Lalu resigns after fodder scam charges; wife Rabri Devi becomes CM

1998 Shahabuddin era begins Siwan Criminal–political nexus Mohammad Shahabuddin consolidates power; symbol of "Jungle Raj"

1999 Shilpi Jain murder case Patna High-profile crime Mysterious deaths of Shilpi Jain and Gautam Singh spark national outrage

2000 Paper leak scandals Patna, Gaya Education / Corruption Major leaks in BPSC & competitive exams; recruitment rigged

2001 IAS officers raise alarm on extortion Statewide Governance breakdown Bureaucrats report political–criminal interference

2002 Attacks on journalists and activists Siwan, Patna Targeted violence Growing impunity of strongmen

2003 Kidnapping crisis peaks North Bihar Organized crime National media brands Bihar "Kidnapping capital of India"

2004 Slow legal action in fodder scam Patna Corruption Trials drag on; political impunity persists

2005 Fall of RJD regime Bihar Political Voters reject Jungle Raj; Nitish Kumar coalition wins

Patterns Seen During the Era

Criminalization of politics: Gangsters turning into legislators and MPs.

State capture: Law-enforcement often neutralized through political pressure.

Economic impact: Flight of capital, industries, and skilled labor.

Administrative decay: Recruitment scams, bribery for postings, and paper leaks.

Social fear: Kidnapping and extortion created a climate of insecurity.

Judicial paralysis: Slow trials, weak witness protection, and low conviction rates.

Legacy of the Jungle Raj

Bihar gained the infamous tag of "lawless state."

Its reputation, investment climate, and migration patterns were shaped for decades.

It also gave rise to public demand for reform, setting the stage for a new political era in 2005.

The cases from this period continue to influence Bihar's politics, courts, and memory.

Chapter 13: The Fall of Institutions — Education and Industry in Decline

For centuries, Bihar had been a land of learning — the home of Nalanda University and Vikramshila University, where students once came from across Asia. But by the late 20th century, that image stood in stark contrast to the ground reality: crumbling schools, paper leaks, ghost teachers, shuttered factories, and young people fleeing the state for survival. The decline was not an overnight collapse — it was a slow institutional erosion, fueled by political apathy, corruption, and lawlessness. This chapter explores how Bihar's once-proud institutions — especially in education and industry — fell apart.

1. Education — From Pride to Collapse

Bihar had produced some of India's greatest scholars, civil servants, and reformers. But by the 1990s, its public education system was on the verge of breakdown:

Infrastructure was in ruins: Many schools had no roofs, toilets, or furniture.

Teacher absenteeism became rampant.

Ghost schools and fake attendance registers were common in rural areas.

Quality of teaching steadily declined.

Rural Education in Ruins In many villages, children attended schools only for the midday meal, not for learning. There were stories of single teachers managing multiple classes or teachers who never came at all.

The collapse of school education created a generation deprived of foundational skills — a reality that still affects Bihar's workforce today.

2. University System in Crisis

Bihar once boasted some of India's oldest universities like Patna University (established 1917), known for academic excellence in its early decades. But by the 1990s and early 2000s, the system had been hollowed out:

Irregular sessions — three-year degrees often took 5–6 years to complete.

Frequent strikes, exam delays, and paper leaks were common.

Political interference in administration was routine.

Universities became power centers for local politicians and strongmen rather than spaces of learning.

This led to an exodus of students to cities like Delhi, Pune, Bangalore, and Kolkata — a migration trend that continues to shape Bihar's demography.

3. Paper Leaks, Cheating Mafia, and "Ghus"

The decline in education was not just about bad infrastructure — it was about systemic corruption:

Paper leaks in competitive exams and board exams became annual scandals.

Cheating mafias operated openly, selling question papers or helping candidates during exams.

Bribery (ghus) became a gateway to government jobs, undermining merit.

Students lost faith in the system, knowing that honest hard work didn't guarantee success.

The impact was devastating: Bihar's youth either migrated for education or were forced into a system that rewarded manipulation, not merit.

4. Decline of Technical and Professional Education

Institutions meant to provide professional training — like engineering, medical, and polytechnic colleges — also suffered heavily:

Lack of qualified faculty.

Poor labs and libraries.

Rampant politicization and corruption in admissions.

Neglect of research and innovation.

Unlike southern states such as Tamil Nadu or Karnataka, which built strong technical universities during the 1990s, Bihar missed the technology wave. This failure further widened the economic gap between Bihar and other regions.

5. The Industrial Collapse

Parallel to the fall of education was the death of Bihar's industrial sector. Once home to major industries, the state witnessed closure after closure from the 1980s onwards.

Examples of Decline:

Bihar State Sugar Corporation units shut down one by one.

The jute industry withered due to mismanagement and lack of modernization.

Fertilizer and engineering plants — like those in Barauni and Dalmianagar — were either shut or ran at a fraction of capacity.

Industrial estates became abandoned ghost zones.

Why It Happened:

Political instability and crime discouraged investment.

Lack of infrastructure — bad roads, power shortage, poor connectivity.

Corruption and bureaucratic red tape made business difficult.

No serious industrial policy or incentives.

The collapse of industry created mass unemployment, particularly in urban and semi-urban areas. Skilled labor migrated to other states, especially Delhi, Punjab, Gujarat, and Maharashtra.

6. Migration — The Escape Route

By the 1990s, migration became a survival strategy for lakhs of Bihari youth. Whether for education, labor, or employment, people began to leave the state in droves.

Students migrated to cities for degrees they couldn't get at home.

Laborers filled factories, farms, and construction sites across India.

Teachers, engineers, and doctors sought stable jobs elsewhere.

This mass migration had two major consequences:

1. It drained Bihar of talent and capital.

2. It built the image of Biharis as migrant workers, not as stakeholders in their own economy.

7. Bureaucratic Decay and Institutional Corruption

The administrative machinery that should have upheld education and industry crumbled under political interference:

Postings and promotions often went to the highest bidder or political loyalists.

Regulatory agencies failed to check corruption.

Public funds meant for development were siphoned off through scams.

Planning and execution were replaced by short-term political appeasement.

Institutions lost credibility, and citizens lost trust.

8. Private Coaching Boom and Parallel Systems

As formal education deteriorated, private coaching centers mushroomed — especially in towns like Patna, Gaya, and Muzaffarpur.

These centers filled the gap left by collapsing schools and colleges.

Many students prepared for exams like Union Public Service Commission, Bihar Public Service Commission, IIT, and medical entrance exams here.

Ironically, this shadow education system thrived on the failure of the state.

While coaching gave opportunities to some, it widened inequality, as poorer students could not afford it.

9. Loss of Intellectual Culture

Bihar had once been known for its intellectual vibrancy — thinkers, poets, and reformers shaped Indian society. But institutional collapse suffocated this intellectual tradition:

Libraries and cultural spaces decayed.

Academic debate gave way to political sloganeering.

University campuses became battlegrounds for local power struggles rather than centers of knowledge.

10. The Economy of Decline

The combined effect of a broken education system and dead industries was catastrophic:

Unemployment soared.

Poverty remained entrenched.

Private investment fled the state.

Bihar became dependent on remittances sent home by migrant workers.

In short, Bihar went from being a proud center of knowledge and enterprise to a state struggling with economic stagnation and a collapsed institutional backbone.

11. The Political Context

This institutional decline cannot be separated from the political climate of the time:

Weak governance and criminalization of politics (as discussed in Chapter 12).

Short-term populism instead of long-term investment.

Neglect of modernization and infrastructure.

Lack of accountability and vision.

Political power became more about identity politics than institutional strengthening.

12. A Glimmer of Change

By the early 2000s, pressure began to build for reform.

Public frustration with corruption and paper leaks grew.

Youth migration became a political issue.

Media coverage of crime and education failures pushed the demand for governance to the center of electoral politics.

This rising pressure set the stage for political change in 2005 — and a new narrative of "sushasan" (good governance) would emerge.

Epilogue to the Chapter

The fall of Bihar's educational and industrial institutions was one of the most devastating long-term consequences of the 1990s era. Crime and corruption were loud, but institutional decay was quiet — a slow rot that hollowed the state from within.

Rebuilding schools, universities, industries, and trust would require not just political will, but a generational effort.

This chapter is not just about the past. It explains why the present looks the way it does — why Bihar remains one of India's largest sources of migrant workers, why its students travel across the country for education, and why its industrial base is still catching up decades later.

Chapter 14: Bihar in Popular Culture

Bihar has long been more than just a geographical entity; it is an emotion, an identity, and a powerful narrative that has found its way into literature, cinema, theater, television, music, and the digital age. The perception of Bihar in popular culture has evolved—sometimes glorified, often misunderstood, but always vibrant and unforgettable. This chapter explores how Bihar has been represented, celebrated, and stereotyped in popular imagination through various mediums over time.

1. The Literary Soul of Bihar

Bihar's cultural legacy is deeply embedded in literature. Long before cinema or television existed, Bihar spoke through poetry, folktales, and classical literature. Ancient texts, such as the teachings of Gautama Buddha and Mahavira, emerged from this land. Later, the intellectual heritage flourished through universities like Nalanda University and Vikramshila University.

In the modern era, Bihar produced some of India's most powerful literary voices. Ramdhari Singh Dinkar, often called the "Rashtrakavi" (national poet), infused nationalism and pride in his poetry, inspiring generations. His work "Rashmirathi" became a symbol of strength and resilience. Phanishwar Nath Renu revolutionized Hindi literature with his novel "Maila Anchal", portraying the rural landscape of Bihar with rare authenticity and emotional depth. His style, often called "anchalik sahitya," created a genre that gave voice to the ordinary people of rural India.

The Bhojpuri language too developed a rich tradition of poetry and songs. Folk ballads sung in fairs and weddings often carried deep social commentary, narrating stories of migration, love, and resistance.

2. Bihar in Bollywood: Between Stereotypes and Stardom

Hindi cinema has often used Bihar as both a setting and a symbol—sometimes of struggle, sometimes of rebellion, and sometimes of humor. Unfortunately, for decades, Bollywood tended to portray Bihar through a narrow lens: as a place of crime, rustic politics, or poverty. This created a national stereotype that Biharis have often had to battle.

Films like Gangaajal (2003) and Apaharan (2005) depicted kidnapping, caste violence, and political nexus, loosely inspired by real incidents in Bihar during the 1990s. While these films were critically acclaimed, they also reinforced a dark image of the state.

However, the tide began to change with the emergence of films that celebrated Bihari identity in more complex and human ways. Manjhi – The Mountain Man (2015), based on the life of Dashrath Manjhi from Gaya, portrayed courage and determination against all odds. Super 30 (2019), inspired by Anand Kumar, highlighted the intellectual potential of the state's youth.

Bihar has also given Bollywood some of its brightest stars—Shatrughan Sinha, Manoj Bajpayee, Sushant Singh Rajput, Neetu Chandra, and Pankaj Tripathi—actors who carried the earthy strength of their land to the national stage. Their rise reflected a change in how Bihar was perceived—not just as a place of problems, but as a land of talent and resilience.

3. Bhojpuri Cinema: A Cultural Powerhouse

Bhojpuri Film Industry, often called "Bhojiwood," emerged in the 1960s and grew into one of India's most vibrant regional film industries. The first Bhojpuri film Ganga Maiya Tohe Piyari Chadhaibo (1962) was a massive hit and marked the beginning of a cultural wave. These films spoke directly to the migrant Bihari population across India and abroad, providing entertainment that reflected their language, humor, traditions, and struggles.

While the industry faced criticism in later years for excessive glamour and formulaic plots, its influence remains undeniable. Superstars like Manoj Tiwari, Ravi Kishan, and Khesari Lal Yadav turned Bhojpuri cinema into a mass movement, connecting Biharis from Patna to Mumbai, Delhi, and even the Caribbean and Fiji.

Bhojpuri songs, especially those tied to festivals, weddings, and migration, became cultural glue for the diaspora. Tracks about homesickness, seasons, and family bonds are still deeply emotional for Biharis living outside their state.

4. Theater and Street Performances

Long before cinema, Bihar had a thriving tradition of nautanki (folk theater) and Bidesiya plays. Bhikhari Thakur, often called the "Shakespeare of Bhojpuri," revolutionized folk theater with his satirical and emotional plays highlighting social issues like dowry, migration, and women's rights. His character "Bidesiya" became symbolic of the migrant Bihari man—torn between his home village and city livelihood.

Even today, Bidesiya performances and street plays are used as tools for social awareness campaigns across rural Bihar. This form of storytelling is a testament to how culture remains a living, breathing entity among ordinary people.

5. Music: The Voice of the Soil

Music is the heartbeat of Bihari culture. From devotional Chhath songs to Bhojpuri Holi numbers, music reflects both faith and festivity. Chhath Puja songs, sung mostly by women, have a deep spiritual resonance and have become popular across India.

Folk instruments like dholak, bansuri (flute), and nagara have remained central to celebrations. Modern artists have fused these traditional sounds with contemporary beats, making Bhojpuri music globally recognizable. Bihari migration has carried these songs to places like Mauritius, Fiji, Suriname, and Trinidad, where Bhojpuri-speaking communities still celebrate their ancestral roots.

6. Bihar on Television and OTT Platforms

Television of the 1990s rarely featured Bihar except in the context of politics or crime. But the new era of digital streaming changed that. Web series and OTT platforms began portraying layered stories about Bihar, offering more than stereotypes.

Shows like Panchayat—though set in a fictional village—captured the humor, innocence, and administrative chaos familiar to rural Bihar. Crime thrillers like Rangbaaz and Khakee: The Bihar Chapter explored real incidents from the state's turbulent years in the 1990s and early 2000s. These narratives gave national audiences a closer, more nuanced look at Bihar's complex socio-political landscape.

7. Migration and Identity in Pop Culture

Bihari identity has been deeply shaped by migration. Millions of people from Bihar travel to metropolitan cities for education, work, or better opportunities. Over time, this created a cultural tension between pride in one's roots and the struggle against discrimination outside the state.

Popular culture captured this journey vividly. In plays, songs, and films, the "Bhaiya" character became both a stereotype and a symbol of resilience. Migrant workers built cities, powered industries, and yet often faced ridicule. But they also held on to their language, festivals, and sense of community, which slowly shifted perceptions.

Today, young creators from Bihar are using platforms like YouTube, Instagram, and X (formerly Twitter) to share their stories, humor, and dialect with pride. This digital revolution has made Bihari identity more visible and celebrated than ever.

8. Satire, Stand-up, and Modern Expression

A new generation of Bihari comedians, storytellers, and satirists has emerged, blending sharp wit with cultural commentary. Stand-up acts and reels often poke fun at everyday life—strict parents, railway journeys, Chhath celebrations, or Bihari accents—turning local experiences into relatable humor.

This light-hearted cultural assertion is powerful. It allows Biharis to reclaim their narrative from old stereotypes and showcase their intelligence, humor, and emotional depth.

9. The Global Bihari Diaspora

Bihar's cultural influence extends far beyond India. The Bhojpuri-speaking diaspora in Mauritius, Fiji, Guyana, Suriname, and Trinidad is living proof of how migration in the 19th century left a permanent cultural mark. Festivals like Chhath are celebrated in Port Louis and Suva with the same devotion as in Patna or Muzaffarpur.

Diaspora communities have also contributed to Bhojpuri music and films, funding projects and creating cultural platforms that keep Bihar alive in distant lands. This global Bihari identity is now shaping how the world sees the state—not just through its problems but its resilience and cultural richness.

10. Stereotypes vs. Reality: Changing the Narrative

For a long time, popular culture outside Bihar painted the state as lawless, backward, and poor. But over the years, especially in the 2010s and 2020s, the narrative has begun to shift. Cinema, literature, and digital media are now telling stories of Bihari engineers, poets, revolutionaries, reformers, and dreamers.

The success stories of personalities like Satyajit Ray's influences on cinema through Patna's intellectual culture, or IAS toppers from Bihar making headlines, have contributed to a more balanced image. Youth are reclaiming their identity with pride, often using the phrase: "Bihari hoon, garv hai!" (I'm Bihari, and I'm proud).

11. Patna: The Cultural Heartbeat

Patna has always been the cultural capital of Bihar. From theaters to book fairs, film festivals, poetry readings, and music concerts, the city has remained a melting pot of traditional and modern expressions. Annual events like the Patna Literature Festival have drawn attention to Bihari writers and thinkers, helping bridge the gap between local talent and national recognition.

Street art and murals are now emerging across cities like Patna, Gaya, and Bhagalpur, depicting historical figures like Chanakya, Ashoka, and Gautama Buddha—reminding everyone that Bihar's cultural story is thousands of years old.

12. Bihari Humor and Memes

In the age of the internet, humor spreads faster than news. Memes using Bihari accents, idioms, or political references have become a subculture in themselves.

Creators cleverly mix sarcasm, wit, and reality—often making viral content that both entertains and educates.

Interestingly, this humorous portrayal has also softened how people outside Bihar perceive Biharis. Laughter, after all, is a powerful bridge.

13. Sports and Cultural Pride

While cricket dominates Indian popular culture, Bihar has also found ways to express its identity through sports. Traditional games like kabaddi and wrestling have long roots in Bihari villages. Modern athletes from Bihar are now emerging in athletics, shooting, and boxing, inspiring young generations and adding new dimensions to cultural identity.

Stadium chants, local tournaments, and school competitions often double as cultural gatherings where food, songs, and pride blend seamlessly.

14. From Ashoka to OTT: A Cultural Continuum

From the Buddhist chants of ancient times to trending reels on Instagram, Bihar's culture has traveled an extraordinary distance. What makes it unique is its adaptability—holding on to its roots while embracing change. Popular culture has both misrepresented and celebrated Bihar, but the people have continued to tell their own stories.

This cultural continuity is what gives Bihar its strength. Even when political or economic narratives falter, its culture remains unbroken.

Conclusion: Owning the Narrative

Bihar in popular culture is a story of two halves: one written by outsiders and one told by Biharis themselves. For a long time, the former dominated. But today, thanks to literature, cinema, music, and digital media, Biharis are reclaiming their identity proudly and powerfully.

The real Bihar is neither the caricature of a lawless land nor a forgotten backwater. It is a land of storytellers, poets, dreamers, rebels, and believers. Popular culture is finally beginning to reflect that truth.

Chapter 15: Modern Bihar — Hopes, Challenges and Rebuilding

Bihar today stands at a crossroads between its glorious past and a future full of possibilities. Once the seat of power, knowledge, and culture, the state has endured centuries of political neglect, economic underdevelopment, and migration. Yet, beneath these layers of struggle lies a pulse of hope—a population determined to rewrite its story.

This chapter explores the journey of modern Bihar—its transformation, its battles, its aspirations, and its people who refuse to give up.

1. A New Century, An Old Struggle

When India entered the 21st century, Bihar was widely seen as the country's most underdeveloped state. Years of political instability, corruption, and weak infrastructure had turned what was once a center of civilization into a symbol of backwardness.

But beneath the headlines, something was changing. The state, under pressure from its youth and civil society, began to inch toward reforms. The challenges remained massive: roads in disrepair, unreliable electricity, collapsing education systems, and a health sector gasping for survival.

The real change, however, was in the aspiration of its people. Migration for survival slowly began to turn into migration for opportunity.

2. Governance and Political Shifts

The political landscape of Bihar in the 2000s and 2010s saw major transformations. After the long rule of Lalu Prasad Yadav and the decline of the so-called "Jungle Raj," a new narrative began to emerge.

In 2005, Nitish Kumar came to power, promising "sushasan" (good governance). Roads were rebuilt, law and order was strengthened, and the state attempted to restore public confidence. The contrast with the previous era was stark—especially in cities like Patna, Gaya, and Muzaffarpur, where visible development began to emerge.

Law and order: Kidnappings for ransom, once common, declined sharply.

Infrastructure: Thousands of kilometers of rural roads were constructed under various schemes.

Electricity: 24x7 power in towns and improved rural electrification became a reality in many areas.

Governance: A focus on administrative reforms and e-governance began to change how people interacted with the state.

Despite these efforts, political challenges remained: shifting alliances, caste-based politics, and the lack of strong industrial policy slowed down sustained growth.

3. Economic Landscape: Agriculture to Aspirations

Bihar remains primarily an agrarian economy. Over 75% of its population still depends on farming. Rich alluvial soil and rivers like the Ganga River, Kosi River, and Gandak River make it one of India's most fertile regions. Yet, farming has remained underdeveloped due to lack of irrigation, cold storage, and modern technology.

However, the economic engine is shifting:

Service sectors, like telecom, education, healthcare, and retail, have grown significantly.

Small and medium enterprises (SMEs) are emerging in towns.

Construction and infrastructure have provided large-scale employment.

The absence of large industries remains a glaring gap. Unlike Gujarat or Maharashtra, Bihar hasn't yet attracted big manufacturing investments. Power shortages (earlier), red tape, and political unpredictability have been major deterrents.

Yet, remittances from Bihari workers working across India—especially in Delhi, Punjab, Haryana, and the Gulf countries—have become a silent lifeline of the state's economy.

4. Education: From Decline to Revival

For decades, Bihar's education system symbolized collapse: leaking classrooms, unpaid teachers, mass cheating in exams, and plummeting standards. Once home to Nalanda University, it had become a cautionary tale of how institutions fall.

But in the past two decades, there have been signs of revival:

New universities and colleges have opened.

Government schemes improved enrollment rates, especially for girls.

Programs like bicycle distribution for girl students encouraged retention.

Bihar has produced some of the most successful students in national exams—be it Indian Institutes of Technology (IITs), Union Public Service Commission (UPSC), or chartered accountancy. Coaching hubs in Patna and Gaya became launchpads for national ambitions.

Private coaching institutes and teachers—like Anand Kumar of Super 30—brought Bihar's education story back into the limelight. These initiatives became models of how individual effort can counter systemic failure.

5. Migration: The Double-Edged Sword

Migration is perhaps the most defining feature of modern Bihar. Millions leave the state every year to work in construction, transport, factories, agriculture, and services in other states.

While this has provided financial relief to countless families, it has also created:

Brain drain: Talented youth settle elsewhere.

Labor vacuum: Farming communities depend on seasonal workers.

Identity struggles: Migrants often face discrimination and stereotyping outside the state.

Yet, Biharis have built reputations for hard work, resilience, and community solidarity across India and abroad. Festivals like Chhath Puja are now celebrated from Mumbai to Dubai—carrying Bihar's culture far beyond its borders.

6. Infrastructure: Rebuilding the Basics

One of the most visible changes in modern Bihar has been the infrastructure boom:

National highways and rural roads have improved connectivity.

Patna Junction and other railway stations are being modernized.

New bridges like the Digha–Sonpur bridge have reduced travel time drastically.

Several new airports and expressways are under development.

This has also fueled growth in real estate, logistics, and small businesses. Urban centers like Patna are slowly evolving into regional commercial hubs.

However, challenges remain in: Urban planning and drainage (especially during floods and monsoon).

Public transport in smaller towns.

Maintenance of existing infrastructure.

7. Health: A Work in Progress

Bihar's health indicators have historically lagged behind the national average. Maternal and infant mortality rates have been high, and government hospitals often lack sufficient facilities.

However, modern Bihar has seen:

Expansion of primary health centers.

Greater vaccination coverage.

Improved response during epidemics like COVID-19.

Increase in private hospitals and clinics in urban areas.

Programs targeting malnutrition, maternal health, and immunization have begun to make slow but steady impacts.

8. Social Change and Women Empowerment

One of the most significant silent revolutions in modern Bihar has been the rise of women. Government schemes like bicycle distribution, school uniforms, and scholarships drastically increased girls' enrollment in schools.

Women's participation in local governance (panchayats) has increased.

Self-help groups have empowered women financially.

Awareness campaigns around domestic violence, health, and education have brought social change to villages.

Bihar still has a long way to go on gender equality, but the winds of change are real and visible.

9. Floods, Climate, and Environmental Challenges

Every year, Bihar faces the fury of rivers like the Kosi, Gandak, and Bagmati. Floods displace thousands, damage crops, and push vulnerable communities deeper into poverty.

Climate change has worsened:

Irregular monsoons

Increased flood frequency

Soil erosion and crop loss

The government has started flood control projects and embankment strengthening, but long-term solutions require ecological planning, river management, and regional cooperation with Nepal, where many rivers originate.

10. Youth, Jobs, and the New Bihar Dream

Bihar has one of the youngest populations in India. Every year, lakhs of students prepare for government jobs, engineering, medicine, and civil services. Coaching hubs, especially in Patna, are booming industries in themselves.

But unemployment remains a huge challenge:Lack of private sector jobs

Limited industrialization

Overdependence on government recruitment

This has created a culture where competitive exams become a lifeline, not just an option. But it also shows the hunger for opportunity—a key driver for future change.

11. Technology and Digital Bihar

Modern Bihar is no longer cut off from the world. Cheap internet access and mobile penetration have brought a digital revolution:

Students in rural areas prepare for national exams using YouTube and Unacademy.

Farmers get weather and crop information on their phones.

Digital payments have reached villages.

E-governance initiatives have made many public services easier to access. Youth entrepreneurs are building startups in edtech, agriculture, and logistics from Bihar itself.

12. Law, Order, and the Shadow of the Past

One of the defining changes of the 2000s was improved law and order. The kidnapping industry, which terrorized Bihar in the 1990s, was largely dismantled. Roads became safer.

But challenges persist:Organized crime in pockets of the state.

Political interference in policing.

Crimes against women and caste-related violence.

The people of Bihar have grown increasingly vocal against injustice, aided by media and digital platforms.

13. Cultural Revival and Pride

Modern Bihar is witnessing a cultural revival. Youth are rediscovering their heritage—be it through Bhojpuri songs, literature, or the celebration of festivals.

Events like the Patna Literature Festival, local theater movements, and Chhath celebrations in metros have made Bihar's cultural identity visible again.

There is a growing pride among young Biharis who say, "Proud to be Bihari," not defensively, but confidently.

14. The Return of the Diaspora

Many successful professionals of Bihari origin are returning or investing back in the state:

Opening schools, hospitals, or tech startups.

Funding social projects.

Mentoring young talent.

This reverse migration of ideas and investment is one of the most hopeful signs for Bihar's future.

15. Politics, Caste, and the Road Ahead

Caste continues to play a major role in Bihar's political identity. Electoral alliances often reflect social equations rather than purely development agendas. However, with youth becoming more aspirational, there's pressure on political parties to deliver results beyond caste calculations.

Development, education, and jobs are slowly replacing caste identity as decisive electoral issues—especially in urban and semi-urban areas.

16. Vision for the Future

For Bihar to truly rebuild, it must:

Industrialize smartly — with policies attracting ethical investment.

Strengthen education and healthcare — not just in cities but villages.

Modernize agriculture — with storage, irrigation, and market access.

Harness its youth — as builders of the future, not just migrants.

Rebrand itself — as a land of potential, not problems.

The people of Bihar have already shown resilience through centuries of change. With focused leadership and inclusive growth, Bihar can once again reclaim its position as a leading state of India.

Conclusion: A State Rising

Bihar's modern story is not just about numbers—it is about people who refuse to be defined by their past. From students burning the midnight oil in Patna's hostels to farmers battling floods, from migrant workers in distant cities to women in village panchayats—every Bihari carries a piece of the state's future.

Bihar may have been underestimated by many. But history has shown—time and again—that when Bihar rises, it changes India.

Chapter 16: Being a Bihari — Identity, Migration and Pride

1. The Idea of "Being a Bihari"

For centuries, the identity of Bihar has been shaped by a unique mix of history, intellect, struggle, and resilience. From the days of Magadh—when this land was the epicenter of knowledge and power—to the modern era where millions of Biharis live and work across the world, "Bihari" has evolved from a geographical identity to a powerful cultural and emotional marker.

The term "Bihari" is not just a demonym; it carries stories of great emperors, scholars, saints, farmers, laborers, freedom fighters, and dreamers. It represents both the legacy of Nalanda and the resilience of migrant workers building modern cities thousands of kilometers away.

2. The Migration Story: From Fields to Cities

2.1 Colonial Period and Early Migration

The roots of large-scale migration from Bihar can be traced back to the 19th century, when thousands of men and women were sent as indentured laborers to countries like Fiji, Mauritius, Trinidad, Suriname, and Guyana during British rule. These "girmitiyas," as they were called, carried with them their Bhojpuri language, songs, and traditions—planting seeds of Bihari culture in distant lands.

2.2 Post-Independence Migration

After Independence, Bihar's economy began to lag behind other states. Industrial decline, frequent floods, poor infrastructure, and lack of employment opportunities forced people to migrate to cities like Delhi, Mumbai, Kolkata, Surat, and Ludhiana in search of livelihood.

By the late 20th century, Bihari workers were a visible part of India's urban workforce—building roads, working in factories, running shops, driving rickshaws, and later excelling in government jobs and entrepreneurship.

2.3 Modern Diaspora

In the 21st century, migration is no longer only about poverty. Many Biharis have moved to the U.S., U.K., UAE, and other countries as professionals, students, and business owners. This modern diaspora has created a global Bihari identity—rooted in culture but open to new opportunities.

3. Stigma, Stereotypes, and Resistance

For decades, Biharis have faced prejudice and stereotyping in other parts of India. Terms like "Bhaiyya" were often used derogatorily. Migrant workers were sometimes targeted during regional agitations, most notably during the 2008 Maharashtra Navnirman Sena attacks on North Indians.

Bihari students and professionals too faced discrimination—mocked for their accents, clothing, or background. Yet, these experiences also created a shared sense of identity and resilience.

Over time, this stigma gave rise to cultural assertion. Bhojpuri music, Maithili literature, and Magahi traditions began reclaiming their pride. Social media and cinema also helped Biharis tell their own stories, challenging stereotypes with success stories.

4. Language and Culture: The Soul of Bihar

Bihar is home to rich linguistic diversity: Bhojpuri, Maithili, Magahi, Angika, and several tribal dialects. Each language carries its own songs, proverbs, and folk tales.

Bhojpuri songs are now a global phenomenon, played at weddings in Mauritius and New York alike. Lollipop Lagelu, for example, became an internet sensation and introduced Bhojpuri beats to international audiences.

Folk arts like Madhubani painting, Sohrai murals, and Chhau dance are also integral to Bihari identity. Festivals like Chhath Puja unite the community across continents—whether performed on the banks of the Ganga River or in distant cities.

5. Education and UPSC Culture

One of the strongest pillars of Bihari identity is education. For decades, Bihar has produced an extraordinary number of bureaucrats, doctors, engineers, and civil servants. Cities like Patna, Gaya, and Darbhanga became hubs for competitive exam coaching.

The "UPSC culture" of Bihar reflects both ambition and resilience. Families sacrifice everything to support one child's preparation. Even migrant workers in cities often send their children back to Bihar for education—because of the strong academic tradition that persists despite infrastructural challenges.

6. Political Consciousness and Leadership

Bihar has historically been politically aware. From the days of Jayaprakash Narayan's "Total Revolution" to mass movements for social justice in the 1990s, Biharis have not only been participants but often the torchbearers of political change in India.

Bihari migrants too remain deeply connected with politics back home—voting during elections, contributing to campaigns, and participating in debates on governance. This consciousness is a key part of their identity.

7. Pride in Resilience

What makes Bihari identity unique is resilience. Generations of Biharis have grown up hearing stories of poverty, floods, and migration—but also of hard work, dignity, and success against odds. A rickshaw puller's son becoming an IAS officer is not just a dream in Bihar—it's a reality repeated countless times.

This pride is visible during festivals, in songs sung in foreign lands, and in how Biharis support each other in new cities. It is a silent strength born out of shared struggle.

8. Changing Perceptions

The narrative around Biharis has slowly begun to change. From being mocked for backwardness, today Biharis are seen as hardworking, smart, and aspirational. Film stars, politicians, IAS toppers, and tech entrepreneurs from Bihar are reshaping the image of the state.

The pride is also visible in how young people use social media to celebrate their heritage—posting Bhojpuri reels, promoting regional food like Litti Chokha, or sharing success stories in Hindi and English alike.

9. The Youth and Digital Bihar

Bihar's youth are digital natives. They carry their identity with confidence. Many have created online communities to teach languages, preserve oral histories, or mentor aspirants. Platforms like YouTube and Instagram have become tools of cultural revival.

Start-ups, NGOs, and youth-led movements are bringing modern energy to traditional identity. A new Bihar is emerging—rooted in its soil but looking firmly to the future.

10. Pride Without Borders

Perhaps the most striking feature of Bihari identity today is that it is not confined to Bihar. Whether in Mumbai, Dubai, London, or Mauritius—Biharis celebrate Chhath Puja with the same devotion. They carry Bhojpuri in their songs, Maithili in their hearts, and the Ganga in their memories.

This global Bihari identity is both emotional and practical—it connects people across distances, generations, and classes.

Conclusion: Ek Bihari Sab Par Bhari

To be a Bihari is to carry centuries of legacy and yet live in the present with grit and hope. It is to have faced mockery and still smile with pride. It is to travel far but keep your roots alive.

This identity is not just inherited—it's built daily, through hard work, through shared festivals, through language, through resilience.

As Bihar moves forward, its greatest strength is its people—Biharis who refuse to be defined by stereotypes and instead define themselves.

"Bihar sirf ek jagah nahi, ek jazba hai."

"Bihari sirf log nahi, ek soch hai."

Chapter 17: Conclusion — Bihar's Future Path

1. Bihar: A Land of Contrasts

Bihar is a paradox. It is a land where the ruins of Nalanda University stand as silent testimony to a golden age of learning — and where, in the present, students often struggle with crumbling classrooms. It is where Ashoka once preached non-violence and dharma — and where, centuries later, the state struggled with lawlessness and political corruption.

It is a land of ancient glory, colonial exploitation, post-independence neglect, mass migration, and a resilient people. But above all, Bihar is not a story of defeat. It is a story of unfinished potential.

The future of Bihar is not just a government project — it is a collective mission.

2. Recognizing the Weight of History

To chart the future, Bihar must first acknowledge its past — both its brilliance and its pain.

It was the heart of Magadh, a global power.

It gave the world Buddhism, Jainism, and knowledge centers that influenced Asia.

It played a defining role in India's freedom struggle, with leaders like Rajendra Prasad and Jayaprakash Narayan.

It endured long years of poverty, crime, and neglect.

Understanding this timeline helps Bihar see its true capacity — not as a victim, but as a civilizational force capable of resurgence.

3. Governance and Accountability

No state can progress without strong, transparent, and accountable governance. Bihar's future depends on:

Breaking the nexus of corruption and politics that began in the late 20th century and still casts a long shadow.

Empowering local governance through Panchayati Raj and decentralized planning.

Ensuring that development funds reach villages, not middlemen.

Creating a bureaucracy that serves, not controls.

Technology can be a powerful ally here. E-governance, transparent tender systems, and real-time monitoring can minimize leakages and build trust.

4. Education: Reclaiming Nalanda's Legacy

Bihar was once the world's classroom. Its future can be secured only when education becomes its strongest pillar again.

Revamping government schools with proper infrastructure, trained teachers, and modern curriculum.

Investing in technical and vocational education, so youth are employable locally, not forced to migrate.

Expanding institutions like Nalanda University (revived in the 21st century) as global centers of excellence.

Encouraging private-public partnerships to build world-class universities and research hubs.

If Bihar educates its youth well, it can transform its economy within a generation.

5. Economic Transformation: From Migration to Opportunity

Today, millions of Biharis migrate to other states for work. A future-ready Bihar must create opportunities within its borders.

Key areas of focus:

Agriculture modernization: introducing cold chains, irrigation, crop diversification, and agro-industries.

Reviving industries: particularly sugar mills, textiles, and small manufacturing units.

turning Bihar's youth into a skilled Skill development: workforce for 21st-century jobs.

Infrastructure push: better roads, railways, power supply, and digital connectivity.

The state's geographical location — close to Nepal, and with access to river routes like the Ganga River — can make it a trade hub if planned strategically.

6. Law and Order: Never Again Jungle Raj

The scars of the 1990s — an era of kidnappings, extortion, caste violence, and fear — still shape Bihar's psyche. To move forward, the state must ensure crime never rules again.

Strengthening the police and judiciary.

Speedy trials and strict action against organized crime.

Community policing and citizen involvement in safety.

Ensuring that political power is never again used to protect criminals.

A safe Bihar is the foundation of a prosperous Bihar.

7. Culture as Power, Not Ornament

Bihar's rich cultural heritage — Bhojpuri songs, Madhubani painting, Chhath Puja, traditional crafts, and folk theater — is not just a matter of pride. It is also a powerful economic and social resource.

Promoting cultural tourism around Nalanda, Bodh Gaya, Vaishali, and heritage sites.

Supporting local artisans and performers to make culture profitable.

Using festivals and art as tools to unite, not divide, communities.

Culture can heal divisions and build confidence.

8. Women at the Center of Change

The story of Bihar's future cannot be written without its women.

From the silent labor of women in villages to leadership in panchayats and universities, women are already reshaping Bihar quietly.

Future focus:

Education for every girl child.

Safety and justice for women.

Economic empowerment through self-help groups, microfinance, and entrepreneurship.

Leadership opportunities at every level of governance.

When women rise, Bihar will rise.

9. Youth Power and Digital Bihar

Bihar's biggest asset is its youth — intelligent, ambitious, and determined.

A young, connected Bihar can leapfrog decades of underdevelopment if:

Start-ups and innovation ecosystems are supported.

Digital literacy becomes universal.

Youth get a real voice in policy-making, not just token representation. Already, online education platforms, social media communities, and small start-ups are emerging from towns like Patna, Gaya, and Muzaffarpur. This momentum must be supported, not stifled.

10. Migration: From Compulsion to Choice

Migration will always be part of Bihar's story — but the goal is to turn it from helplessness into empowerment.

People should go out to explore, not to survive.

Migrant workers must have legal and social protections.

Government and community organizations can build strong networks to support the diaspora.

Return migration should be encouraged with business opportunities back home.

Bihar's diaspora can be a powerful force for investment, mentorship, and change.

11. A Shared Dream

Bihar's future cannot depend on politicians alone. It must be a collective dream:

Of farmers adopting new methods.

Of teachers shaping brilliant minds.

Of youth leading with vision.

Of migrants returning with pride.

Of citizens demanding accountability.

The strength of Bihar has always been its people. That strength must now be organized, modernized, and mobilized.

12. A New Dawn: From Magadh to Modernity

When the sun rose over ancient Pataliputra, it illuminated the greatest empire of its time. When it rises tomorrow over modern Bihar, it has the potential to illuminate a new model of growth rooted in heritage.

Bihar's journey is not over — it is being rewritten. From being called "backward," it can become an example of how a society can rebuild itself through education, justice, culture, and unity.

"Bihar ek kahani hai — girne ki, uthne ki, aur fir se chamakne ki."

(Bihar is a story — of falling, rising, and shining again.)

"Jis mitti ne Ashoka ko janma diya, us mitti ko koi daba nahi sakta."

(The soil that gave birth to Ashoka cannot be defeated.)

Epilogue: Reflections on Bihar

As I close this journey through the lands of Bihar—from the rise of Magadh to the hopes of modernity—I am struck by one enduring truth: Bihar is more than history, politics, or geography. It is a living story, told through its rivers, its cities, its villages, and most importantly, its people.

Bihar is the soil of empires and saints, of poets and revolutionaries. It has faced invasion, neglect, and disaster, yet it has never lost its heartbeat. Its identity has been tested, often misrepresented, and at times, underestimated—but every generation of Biharis has risen to meet its challenges with resilience, wit, and courage.

What does it mean to write about Bihar today? It is to acknowledge the dual realities of pain and promise. Yes, there were periods of stagnation, political chaos, and social struggle. But there were also moments of brilliance, innovation, and triumph—the kind of brilliance that inspired not just a region, but the world.

This book is not just a chronicle of events. It is a celebration of a people who carry the weight of history on their shoulders and yet dream fearlessly of a better tomorrow. Every child learning under a banyan tree, every farmer toiling in the fields, every student preparing for exams far from home, every artisan painting Madhubani patterns—they are the living testimony of Bihar's undying spirit. The future of Bihar will not be written by governments alone. It will be written by its citizens, its thinkers, its doers, and its dreamers. The soil that nurtured Ashoka, the intellectual vigor of Nalanda, the resilience of migrant workers, and the creativity of its youth—all converge to form a state capable of unparalleled renewal.

If there is a lesson to take from Bihar's journey, it is this: resilience, identity, and hope are stronger than any adversity. Bihar has fallen, Bihar has struggled, but Bihar has always risen. Its story is unfinished, and that is its most powerful promise.

To read about Bihar is to understand not just a state, but a spirit—a spirit that refuses to be defined by misfortune, and instead chooses to define itself by courage, culture, and the unwavering belief in a brighter tomorrow.

"Bihar is not a place you merely live in; it is a legacy you carry, a history you honor, and a future you shape."

www.ingramcontent.com/pod-product-compliance
Lightning Source LLC
Chambersburg PA
CBHW011802160726
48282CB00035B/1239
9789334436679